Environmental Politics: A Very Short Introduction

VERY SHORT INTRODUCTIONS are for anyone wanting a stimulating and accessible way into a new subject. They are written by experts, and have been translated into more than 45 different languages.

The series began in 1995, and now covers a wide variety of topics in every discipline. The VSI library now contains over 500 volumes—a Very Short Introduction to everything from Psychology and Philosophy of Science to American History and Relativity—and continues to grow in every subject area.

Titles in the series include the following:

Andrew Dobson

ENVIRONMENTAL POLITICS

A Very Short Introduction

OXFORD
UNIVERSITY PRESS

Great Clarendon Street, Oxford, OX2 6DP,
United Kingdom

Oxford University Press is a department of the University of Oxford.
It furthers the University's objective of excellence in research, scholarship,
and education by publishing worldwide. Oxford is a registered trade mark of
Oxford University Press in the UK and in certain other countries

Published in the United States of America by Oxford University Press
198 Madison Avenue, New York, NY 10016, United States of America

British Library Cataloguing in Publication Data
Data available

Library of Congress Control Number: 2015951914

ISBN 978-0-19-966557-0

Printed in Great Britain by
Ashford Colour Press Ltd., Gosport, Hampshire.

Contents

Acknowledgements

It has been a privilege and a pleasure to work with so many outstanding scholars during the twenty-five years I have spent researching and writing about environmental politics. It is impossible to thank them all here, but if they read these words they will surely know who they are. In relation to this particular book, I would like to thank two anonymous readers who made valuable suggestions on both the plan for the book and its first draft. Chris Loynes and Lucy Sargisson made important comments on points of detail, while Neil Carter, Brian Doherty, Sherilyn MacGregor, and John Vogler all read specific chapters in the midst of their own busy schedules and helped me to improve the text enormously. I am very grateful both to them and to everyone else in the uniquely supportive environmental politics scholarly community. Finally, I would like to thank Jenny Nugee at OUP for her invaluable editorial suggestions, and Joy Mellor for her excellent copyediting.

Andrew Dobson
May 2015

List of illustrations

List of tables

Introduction: what is environmental politics?

Vignettes

Harris pushed the button on the elevator which would take him up to his room on the top floor of the Pullman Hotel, in the Avenue de Suffren, Paris. He'd asked for a room with a view of the Eiffel Tower and he was looking forward to sitting on the balcony with a glass of wine in his hand as the sun went down. As the elevator door opened he clutched the file in his hand more tightly. 'COP21—Paris, December 2015', said the label. Harris was looking forward to the climate change negotiations. Surely this time they'd crack it. This time they *had* to crack it, he thought, as he turned up the central heating in his room and tossed his used airline ticket in the waste paper bin.

It was dusk, and Hualing looked inside the one-ton sack that had been beside her all day. It was full of plastic bottles from which she'd been removing labels for the last twelve hours. The bottle she held in her hand had been recycled by Harris, in Manchester, a month before. Hualing had come to Beijing from Sichuan Province a few months back, hoping to find better work than the back-breaking labour in her rural village. She turned the bottle over in her hand and wondered if this weary existence was an improvement on life back home. She put the bottle on a pile next to her, reached into the sack, and pulled out the next one to sort, just like the foreman had told her.

Patrick logged on to the Findhorn Foundation website and found what he was looking for: a four-week programme on Applied Ecovillage Living. Ah, Scotland! The programme promised to provide him with the 'concepts, tools and techniques needed for creating sustainable human settlements'. He'd learn about organic food production, deep ecology (whatever that was), ecological building, and permaculture. 'Ecovillage communities are cohesive social structures, united by common social and/or spiritual values', the website told him. 'Working with the simple principle of not taking away more from the Earth than one gives back, ecovillages also consciously keep their ecological footprint to a minimum', it said. He'd always wanted to find a way of reducing his impact on the world, and here was the answer. Patrick checked his bank balance, clicked the 'book online' tab, and began to fill in the questionnaire.

Freda and Carla stepped out into the beautiful spring day—so warm, it felt like summer had already arrived. 'Got the leaflets?' asked Carla. Freda held up her bag with a smile. 'Right here', she said. 'Got around a hundred houses to do', said Carla, 'if you take the left-hand side of the street and I take the right, we should be done in about an hour'. The election was just over two weeks way, and this was a target constituency for the local party. They weren't far off holding the balance of power on the local council. If results went their way, two more seats should do it. 'Local Green Party Opposes Landfill Site', said the leaflet. Carla pushed the first one through the letterbox.

Nanhe misses his cow. He remembered being alarmed when men on bicycles wearing trousers and shirts rode into their villages to speak of the dam. He remembered being excited and frightened when an aircraft flew over his condemned village, carrying out survey work. When he and his wife and two daughters were

2

resettled he knew it would be hard enough to keep them alive, and the cow had to be left behind. He loved his cow so much that he left her with a cowherd and paid a little towards her upkeep until she died ten years later. Now Nanhe sits quietly outside his hut in the resettlement village of Aitma, India, for most of the day. But sometimes when he speaks, he says softly to anyone who is willing to hear: 'When I am on a boat in the middle of the reservoir, and I know that hundreds of feet below me, directly below me, at that very point, lie my village and my home and my fields, all of which are lost forever, it is then that my chest rips apart, and I cannot bear the pain…'

George stood in the field with the hills behind him. 'I'm an environmentalist too!' he said to the radio interviewer. 'If the windfarm goes ahead, this beautiful view, enjoyed by tourists and local people for generations, will be destroyed for ever. These greens call themselves lovers of nature, but all they want to do is cover it with wind turbines. Besides, they make a dreadful noise, they kill birds, and they don't even work very well. We don't want them here, we don't want them anywhere'. Upon which, George turned on his heel, climbed into his hybrid SUV, and drove off into the distance.

What this book is about

Only one of these stories is true, the one involving Nanhe, his cow, and his resettlement. But all of them are recognizable, from the climate change negotiator to the rubbish tip recycler in China; from the individual determined to find ways of reducing his environmental impact to the Green party campaigners; and from Nanhe to the opponent of windfarms. Each of these vignettes represents a face of environmental politics, and there are many more besides. Up until quite recently these stories would have been literally unthinkable—environmental politics is a new politics, and it is still finding its feet. This new politics has a history, though, and we start with the most remote origins of environmental concern and trace its acceleration and deepening up to the present day. We then move on to the ideas that lie behind environmental politics and some of the disputes that take place in it. Why should we care about the environment? We obviously have practical reasons for doing so, because air, water, and soil are the foundations of our wellbeing. But do other species deserve our care and attention even if they are not useful to us? If so, why? If not, why not? We also discuss the differences between environmental politics and other types of politics. What is it about the environmental politics message that makes it stand out in today's political market place, and how have other types of politics reacted?

We continue by looking at the practice of environmental politics, the movement and the parties that enact it, and the policy tools that governments use. The history of the movement is discussed, as well as the question of the different forms it takes, and how unified it is. The birth and development of Green parties around the world is described, and their effectiveness is debated. Environmental problems are complex and sometimes seem intractable, and we outline the range of policy options open to governments when they grapple with these problems. Many environmental issues are, by their very nature, international issues, and we engage with this dimension of environmental politics by discussing the nature and environmental impact of globalization, together with a brief history of multilateral environmental agreements. What makes the negotiations that lead these agreements successful? What makes them fail? These questions are explored through comparing ozone diplomacy with climate change diplomacy. It is too simple to think of the world as divided into the 'national' and 'international' and the 'global North' and the 'global South', though. These scales interpenetrate, and the idea of environmental justice is used to discuss the way in which environmental politics can be understood as the securing of livelihoods.

We conclude by looking to the future of environmental politics, using the background of the enormous changes wrought on the earth by human activity over the past 200 years as a frame. There are some who say that these changes have produced a whole new geological epoch: the Anthropocene. We are the custodians of this new era. How should we discharge this enormous responsibility, both to ourselves and to the future? Is it a case of business-as-usual, or all change?

Chapter 1
Origins

Climbing ropes used to be a standard 45 metres long. By some cosmic coincidence, the Earth is reckoned to be 4.54 billion years old, which means that every metre on the rope represents roughly 100 million years of Earth history.

If you were to lay the rope out and mark some key moments on it, you'd find that free oxygen first appeared in the Earth's atmosphere around the 23-metre mark—just over half way along the rope. The first animals appear at around 33 metres, and the first dinosaurs at 43 metres—very near the end of the rope. The first hominids (*genus Homo*) appear just 2.3 millimetres from the end of the rope. That's the width of about twenty pages, looked at end-on, of the book you are holding in your hand.

One thing that is clear from this is that the Earth has been around for much longer than we have, and in its guise as the third rock from the sun there's very little we can do to halt its march through the heavens. But we are a force to be reckoned with when it comes to the Earth as a home for human beings and the nine billion other species with which we share it. For 99 percent of our time on Earth—99 percent of those 2.3 millimetres—humans lived a hunting and gathering existence which impacted very little on the environment around them. Whatever impact there was would have been relatively minor and short-lived, and the environment's recovery from the effects of nomadic human life was generally rapid and complete.

Most of our impact has therefore been in the last one percent of the last 2.3 millimetres of the 45-metre rope that represents the history of the Earth. So what has happened in that infinitesimally small slice of our time on Earth to give rise to a politics of the environment?

Agriculture

It is generally recognized that there have been two major moments of acceleration of human impact on the world around us, neither of which heralded a politics of the environment as such, but both of which increased the intensity of our impact. In doing so they laid the foundations for concern about the sustainability of ways of life, a concern which is central to environmental politics.

The first of these moments (though in truth it was less a 'moment' and more a process that lasted several thousand years) was the development of agriculture, which began about 12,000 years ago. Humans have long interacted with plants and animals for their sustenance, and the difference between hunting and gathering and farming is one of degree rather than of kind—though it is a difference that has an effect as far as the potential for intensity of impact is concerned. So hunter-gatherers follow herds and forage for plants and fruit, while farmers close-herd their animals and plant and cultivate deliberately. The main advantage farmers have is that they are able to extract more food from a smaller area. It is not clear that farming is an easier way of providing food than hunting and gathering, and this raises the question of why people started to farm in the first place. It is possible that it was a response to population pressures in localized areas where the land was no longer able to support a nomadic existence.

Either way, agriculture gave rise to two phenomena that lie at the heart of contemporary environmental concerns. The first is the intensification of the impact of human activity on the environment, and the question of how sustainable that activity is over the long term. Growing food on the same piece of land over a long period of time can lead to a deterioration of the land, and this can put its long-term future as a source of food in doubt. This is a problem of environmental *sustainability*. Environmentalists say that many of the issues we have to deal with today, like global warming—or climate change (the terms will be used indistinguishably)—have the same structure: human activity puts pressure on the environment to the point where its capacity to sustain a comfortable and relatively predictable life cannot be guaranteed. Farmers develop techniques to keep their land fertile, ranging from crop rotation, to organic fertilizers, to chemical fertilizers, and to genetic engineering. More generally, environmental politics is in part about the search for solutions to unsustainability and putting them into practice. So solutions for global warming run from rationing people's carbon emissions, to better house insulation, to giant mirrors in orbit around the Earth to reflect the sun's rays back into space.

And this introduces the second issue: how sustainable are these solutions to unsustainability? If it was indeed the case that agriculture was a response to population pressures, then it might just have sidestepped the problem rather than eradicated it. This is because agriculture allowed settled communities to develop and populations to grow, further intensifying impact. So, arguably, the solution to the problem simply made it worse. Similarly, some will say that giant mirrors in space deflect (literally) the problem rather than get to the root cause of it—the root cause being a continuous rise in greenhouse gas emissions from human activity.

Industry

The second moment of acceleration of human impact on the environment occurred about 10,000 years after the development

CHINA MAKING AT STOKE-ON-TRENT

1. Pollution from pottery kilns in 19th-century Stoke-on-Trent (UK).

of the first agricultural communities—the Industrial Revolution (see Figure 1). Up to about the mid-18th century, human societies lived mainly off the energy available from the sun on a daily, weekly, monthly, seasonal basis. This is known as the flow of energy, which is different from the stock of energy. The stock of energy is what is stored up over a period of time—such as the energy in the wood in a tree. Energy stocks are very useful because they enable more work to be done in a shorter period of time than is possible with just the flow of energy.

It is helpful to think of this kind of energy as 'stored sunlight'. Some of this sunlight has been stored for a short period of time—like the wood in a tree, for example. This takes us back no more than a few decades into the storehouse. Other sunlight, in the form of coal and oil, has been stored for much longer—millions of years. Very small amounts of coal have been used for domestic purposes since about 3500 BC (in China), and the Romans used it extensively in Britain during their long occupation. Wherever it has been easily accessible it has been used, but it was not until we began to mine and burn coal systematically in the middle of the

9

18th century, and, about a hundred years later in 1850, to extract petroleum, that we began seriously to deplete the sunlight storehouse—with two main consequences that have contributed to the rise of environmental politics.

The first consequence is a concern about resources, and the second relates to the unintended consequences of our actions. It would be wrong to say that environmental politics is only about resource use, but it is certainly a big part of this kind of politics. More particularly, there is an important distinction between renewable and non-renewable resources. Fossil fuels are non-renewable resources, which are therefore finite. Finite resources will, by definition, run out at some point. This brings the issue of sustainability back into view. Much of what we have achieved over the past 250 years has been made possible by the use of fossil fuels, but if these are due to run out then the sustainability of the civilization that relies on them must be in question. One possible solution is to replace a non-renewable resource with another—uranium for oil, for example. This would give us nuclear energy rather than fossil-fuelled energy. This might buy us some time, but it would not be a sustainable solution in the long term—unless technological advances were made that could spin out the viability of nuclear energy far into the future. Debates over the degree to which technology can help us meet the challenge of sustainability are indeed a key element in environmental politics. There are, though, those who argue that unsustainability is more a political than technological problem, more to do with how we organize our lives and what we expect out of them than about the application of science. These critics doubt the capacity of the 'technological fix' to solve our sustainability problems, and argue instead for changes in the behaviour and objectives of individuals and organizations along sustainability principles.

Another solution to the energy problem is to make a move to renewable resources. The advantage of renewables is that they never run out, but a potential disadvantage is that, from an energy point of view, it is unclear whether they can power the lifestyles that so-called developed societies have become accustomed to. So is there a trade-off between sustainability and prosperity? Will high-energy societies always be unsustainable societies? These are the kinds of questions that make environmental politics unlike any other politics. There is no other politics that concerns itself centrally with the relationship between humans and their environment, and with the question of how to regulate that relationship so it is sustainable over the long term.

The second feature of the Industrial Revolution which has had an impact on the development and nature of environmental politics is a growing realization of the potential force of the unintended consequences of our actions. When we first started burning coal and oil no-one suspected that a build-up of CO_2 in the atmosphere would lead to a rise in average global temperature—this was an unintended consequence of the burning of fossil fuels. Many of our actions have unintended consequences, of course, but as the scale of our impact on our environment grows, the potential for harm caused by these consequences increases correspondingly. As well as increasing and accelerating the intensity of our impact on the environment, the Industrial Revolution also broadened the potential scope of that impact. As societies and civilizations grew, in great part as a result of the development of agriculture discussed earlier, their impact grew. There is evidence that some of these societies collapsed as a result of resource overuse—examples often cited are the Mayan civilization of Latin America in the 8th and 9th centuries AD, and Easter Island in the Pacific Ocean in the mid-18th century. These examples are contested, and the Easter Island collapse, for example, is sometimes put down to disease brought in by European visitors rather than unsustainable resource use.

Be that as it may, these are examples of unintended consequences and, while they were obviously disastrous for the people concerned, the impacts were only felt at a 'local' level. What is striking about the Industrial Revolution is that it gave rise to an unintended consequence with a global reach—global warming. No other species has the capacity to affect the planet as a whole, and it took the human species until now to realize this potential. This is why the Industrial Revolution is such a significant historical moment in the development of environmental politics—and particularly the possibility of a global environmental politics. So far-reaching has human impact on the environment become, indeed, that it has been suggested that we have set in train a whole new geological epoch—the 'Anthropocene'. We will look at this claim and its implications in more detail in Chapter 5.

Revolution and reaction

The Industrial Revolution was itself made possible in part by the intellectual revolution that took place in Europe around the 18th century—the Enlightenment. The Enlightenment saw a burgeoning of the scientific method, and of the belief in the capacity of rational thought to explain the workings of the natural world. For some scientists of the time like Francis Bacon this translated into the ambition to control nature, and to submit it (or 'her' as he referred to it) to the will of human beings. Once people began to look for the causes of our environmental problems in the contemporary era, this attitude of domination looked as though it could be part of the problem, as it set nature apart from human beings and constructed it as an enemy to be conquered.

In the 19th century there was a reaction in Europe to the Industrial Revolution which went (and goes) by the name of Romanticism, and Romanticism has played a role in the development of contemporary environmental politics. Romantics in the 19th century railed against what they saw as the ugliness of industrialization and the way in which the primal forces of nature were being subdued by the rational mind and actions of 'man'. Around this time, ideas of the 'noble savage' were popular among Romantics, a person unsullied by the modern world and instinctively in tune with the natural world. There were also concerns about scientists 'playing God' with nature and suffering the consequences. This is the theme of Mary Shelley's *Frankenstein*, whose alternative title is—evocatively—'The Modern Prometheus'. Prometheus, it will be remembered, was the Titan who stole fire from Zeus and was punished for it. This warning against humans overreaching their 'natural' capacities has its echoes today in the belief among some in the environmental movement that our problems are caused by too much of a separation between nature and human beings—that we see ourselves as *apart from* rather than a *part of* the natural world. Sometimes this view is accompanied by a harking back to the hunter-gatherer period of human existence, as a time at which humans and nature were in harmony with one another. From this point of view, the agricultural and industrial epochs drove a progressively deep wedge between humans and nature, and the surest way of healing the rift, it is sometimes said, is to draw on the well of Romanticism that sees humans as part of nature.

The same century saw the development of a scientific route to a similar conclusion regarding humans' relation to nature, and it is important to recognize this early contribution of science to environmentalism since science plays a key role in contemporary environmental politics. In 1859, Charles Darwin published *On the Origin of Species*, where he showed that the present diversity of life is caused by evolution and natural selection, and that humans are descended from apes. This challenged the dominant view in Christianity that humans are made in the image of God and are fundamentally different to the rest of 'creation'. Thus Darwin reached the same conclusion as the Romantics by a different route—that humans are a part of nature rather than apart from it.

Darwin's work had a related effect that has influenced the development of environmental politics—a 'decentring' of the human being. Back in 1543 Copernicus had published *De revolutionibus orbium coelestium* (*On the Revolution of the*

Celestial Spheres), in which he argued that the Earth goes round the Sun rather than vice versa. This was an early intimation that the Earth and the humans who live on it are not special—confirmed by Darwin's account of humans being descended from apes. In this same century, Ernst Haeckel first used the word 'ecology', intended to designate the science of the study of the relationships between organisms rather than their location in a hierarchy. This served to emphasize the interdependence of organisms—including the human organism—on one another. All these developments helped to destabilize the dominant view of 'human exceptionalism', the idea that the world was made for the benefit of human beings, and the related view that humans had a right to do whatever they wanted to it.

In one sense, though, human exceptionalism is an important feature of contemporary environmental politics. It is generally believed that the human animal is the only animal that can systematically (as opposed to occasionally) reflect on the world around it, act 'beyond instinct', and make meaningful, long-term choices. This gives us the capacity to understand the causes of environmental problems, develop policies to deal with them, and put those policies into action. Thus the Enlightenment and the 19th century gave us some of the key building blocks for today's environmental politics: a series of environmental problems rooted in industrialization, the capacity to analyse those problems and devise solutions to them, and an ambivalent view as to whether these solutions entail more or less of an attempt to control the world around us.

The long 19th century

These 19th-century developments are bracketed by two further legacies which have left an enduring mark on today's environmental politics: the idea of scarcity, and the first stirrings of a politics of energy. In the midst of a century of burgeoning plenty—even if very unequally shared—Thomas Malthus' argument in his *An Essay on the Principle of Population* that population multiplies geometrically and food arithmetically, and so population will eventually outstrip the food supply, struck an unusual chord. Malthus' point was that scarcity is a fundamental feature of the human condition rather than a temporary or contingent issue that can be overcome. This was a direct challenge to the Enlightenment idea, embodied in political theories such as Marxism, that things would always get better, and this challenge resurfaced in the 1970s in the guise of the important 'limits to growth' thesis which we will look at shortly.

Energy has come to be a fundamental issue in environmental politics, especially in regard to debates over renewable and non-renewable forms, the desirability of nuclear energy, disputes over the siting of wind turbines, and so on. Whatever its source, energy is fundamental to our lives, and, therefore, from a 'green' point of view, to our politics. This was first pointed out by the German chemist, Wilhelm Ostwald, in the late 19th century, who argued that we can do nothing without energy, and he developed an overarching theory that explained the development of human civilization in terms of the control of energy for human purposes. The idea was taken up by, among others, Frederick Soddy, English Nobel Prize winning radiochemist, who created an economic theory based on the laws of thermodynamics, representing a set of non-negotiable physical limits within which any politics or economics must operate. Once again, the notion of limits was taken up in the 1970s and has come to be a key—if disputed—reference point in contemporary environmental politics.

The idea that human possibilities are limited by circumstance and capacity is generally taken to be sign of conservatism, of right-wing thinking. We tend, today, to associate environmentalists with the left of the political spectrum, but it is important to note that in the early part of the 20th century some 'back to the land' movements in Europe were associated with the right. This is because 'the land' was seen in terms of the land of a particular nation rather than land in general, so looking after the land, being rooted in it, amounted to a defence of the nation and its culture and history. Thus the 'environmentalists' of this period were often conservatives and nationalists.

The 1960s and 1970s

There will always be disputes about when environmental politics 'properly speaking' began, but if we think of it as a jigsaw, then some time around the 1960s and 1970s the pieces began to come together: a growing awareness that negative environmental impacts might be a result of a mistaken whole development path, rather than local and isolated difficulties; and a political movement coalescing around those problems, offering an alternative political platform. One key moment in this process was the publication of Rachel Carson's book *Silent Spring*, about the impact of agricultural pesticides on the environment. The title of the book evokes the silence that would result from declining bird populations from pesticide poisoning—a picture that captivated large swathes of the American people, exposing them to environmental concerns as never before. A second moment was on 24 December 1968, when astronaut William Anders took the famous 'Earthrise' photograph from Apollo 8 as it swung round from behind the moon (see Figure 2). This picture captured the vulnerability of the blue, green, and white planet Earth as it hung in the blackness of space—an image that has adorned many a book cover, NGO logo, and PowerPoint presentation since.

A third crucial moment was the publication of *The Limits to Growth* report in 1972 (updated in 1992 and 2004). A key theme of this chapter, and of environmental politics in general, is how best to make use of the resources available to us. Underlying that question is another one: are these resources limited or not? This is a complicated question which we will explore further in Chapter 2, but the basic thesis of the 'Limits' team is that infinite growth in a finite system is impossible. The finite system in question is the Earth (whose finitude is graphically depicted in the

2. 'Earthrise' photograph taken from Apollo 8, 24 December 1968.

Apollo 8 Earthrise photograph), and the infinite growth refers to an infinitely growing economy. The idea that there might be limits to how far an economy can grow puts environmental politics on a collision course with most mainstream politics, where a growing economy (increasing gross domestic product—GDP) is regarded as a sign of success.

Another important feature of the 'Limits' report was that it analysed the global system as a whole. A common feature of the environmental and resource problems encountered throughout human history up until the last half century or so is that they were local and/or regional. We saw that resource scarcity might have been the reason for the collapse of the Mayan and Easter Island civilizations, among others, but, however disastrous this was for the Mayans and the Easter Islanders, the causes and consequences of collapse were confined to those regions. There were always more resources 'somewhere else'. The lesson from *The Limits to Growth* is that—barring interplanetary travel—there is no 'somewhere else' as far as resources, and space to grow food and accommodate waste are concerned. Around this time, Kenneth Boulding coined the term 'Spaceship Earth' to convey the idea of a self-contained system, wholly reliant for its survival on what it carries with it and unable to count on outside help. These thoughts raised the stakes as far as our relationship with our environment is concerned, making it clear to some that the margin for error was getting increasingly small—a concern which has a particular and pressing form in the shape of global warming.

But all these are 'merely' ideas. Politics needs people to enact these ideas in the political arena, and two rather different mobilizations have taken place, giving rise to contrasting types of environmental politics. The first is described by the so-called 'post-material' thesis, most thoroughly developed by Ronald Inglehart. According to this thesis, as societies become more materially affluent, their members are freed from having to spend all their time satisfying their basic needs, and have the time and resources to devote to post-material values such as autonomy and self-expression. Environmental concerns are sometimes regarded as a 'luxury extra', to be attended to once more pressing and material concerns have been dealt with—an ideal issue area to attract Inglehart's post-materialists.

On this reading a precondition for the development of environmental politics is material affluence, but there is a very different type of environmental politics which is rooted in the opposite circumstance: material deprivation, and livelihoods threatened by environmental damage and destruction. It is often said that post-material environmentalism is characteristic of the global North, while livelihood environmentalism is typical of the global South. (The terms 'global North' and 'global South' are only partly geographical; here they refer to the distinction between developed and developing countries—so Australia is counted as a member of the 'global North' even though it lies in the southern hemisphere). While this is accurate up to a point, it is also true to say that there are post-materialists in the global South (the burgeoning middle-classes of India and China, for example) and people in the global North whose livelihoods are threatened by environmental degradation (living near toxic waste dumps, for example). We will look more closely at these different kinds of environmental politics in Chapter 4.

All of this strongly suggests that the 1970s is an important decade when it comes to locating the origins of environmental politics, and the hypothesis is strengthened by the observation that many of the best-known international environmental organizations and Green political parties were founded around this time. There are often disputes about the exact dates of the founding of organizations, since the names by which they have come to be known are not always the names of the groups from which they emerged. Bearing that in mind, we can say that Friends of the Earth was founded in 1969, and Greenpeace in 1972, while the two parties that vie for the accolade of 'first Green party', in Tasmania and New Zealand (the United Tasmania Group and the Values Party, respectively) were both founded in 1972. Perhaps the best-known Green party of all, *die Grünen*, the German Greens, held its first party congress in 1980, and made a breakthrough in the Federal elections in 1983 when it won 5.6 percent of the vote and twenty-seven seats in the Bundestag. This showed other Green parties that electoral success was a real possibility, and since then Green representatives have been elected to public office at local, regional, national, and international level in many countries around the world. We will look at these developments, and analyse the factors that make for Green party electoral success and failure, in some detail in Chapter 3.

We started with a rope 45 metres long, representing the 4.54 billion-year history of the Earth. Human impact on the Earth occupies about 1 per cent of the last 2.3 millimetres of that rope, and our discussion in this chapter shows that environmental politics has been with us for a tiny fraction of that 1 per cent. In that short space of time it has made a dramatic impact on the political landscape in many ways and at many levels. The rest of this book is devoted to exploring, explaining, and discussing this impact, with Chapter 2 being about the ideas underpinning it.

Chapter 2
Ideas

In an obvious way, environmental politics is about our relationship with the environment. We saw in Chapter 1 how human impact on the environment has increased over the millennia—to the point where, over the past fifty years or so, that impact has come to seem to threaten everything from local livelihoods to global weather patterns. So if we were to ask ourselves why we should care for our environment, the answer might be: because a healthy and functioning environment is fundamental to human wellbeing. This is probably the most common answer given to that question, but it is not the only one. If environmental politics is about our relationship with the environment, then environmental ethics is about the different reasons we can give for looking after it, and later in the chapter we will see how different these reasons can be. First, though, we will focus on what we might call the practical reasons for environmental concern.

The environment as 'life-support', and 'limits to growth'

From this practical point of view, the environment is sometimes described as a 'life-support system'. There are two ways of looking at this—or two 'scales'—and these tend to correspond to the two sites of environmentalist practice that we encountered in Chapter 1. In the 'close up' view, the environment is a source of immediate sustenance, and environmental problems are experienced as a threat to day-to-day livelihoods. This is sometimes called an 'environmentalism of the poor' (this influential term was coined by Joan Martínez-Alier), and while it is usually associated with the global South, or the 'majority countries', this can be misleading. In the first place, not all people in the global South are poor. In countries like China, India, Indonesia, and Brazil there is a rapidly expanding middle-class which no longer has the immediate connection with environmental problems that drives the environmentalism of the poor. To the extent that they have environmental concerns, they are likely to be rooted in the bigger scale problems we are about to discuss. The second reason is that there are poor people in the global North, or 'minority countries', as well. These people are usually at the heart of what has come to be known as the 'environmental justice' movement, and they are mobilized to action by catastrophic breakdowns in environmental conditions that threaten their health and safety. We will look at some examples of these mobilizations in Chapters 3 and 4, but what links the poor in the global North and South in environmental terms is the immediacy of the impact of environmental breakdown on their lives.

This contrasts with the other scale—the 'long-distance' view—in which environmental problems seem distant in space and time. Classic examples of such problems might be global warming, or nuclear waste. In this long-distance view, we can once again conjure up the image of the blue-and-white Earth hanging in space, containing all the resources, air, and water that we will ever have. As we saw towards the end of Chapter 1, alarm bells began ringing some fifty years ago with the publication of books like Rachel Carson's *Silent Spring*, but it was not until the publication of *The Limits to Growth* in 1972 that the long-term future of the Earth as a life-support system for human beings was put into question. The report was commissioned by the Club of Rome, a think-tank researching international issues, and the report's authors were predominantly system dynamics experts. The report consisted of a computer simulation of the world system, plotting five 'trends of global concern' in various different scenarios. The five trends were: industrial output per capita, food per capita, population, depletion of non-renewable resources, and pollution. The first scenario the team ran through the computer was 'business-as-usual'—i.e., the way the global economy was being run in the early 1970s—and in this scenario the system collapsed because it ran out of non-renewable resources in about 2100.

A common response in the face of concerns that we might run out of resources is to say that either more resources will be found or we can extend the life of our resource base by using them more efficiently, or some combination of the two. To test this response, the research group assumed a doubling of resources in the next computer run, but without altering any of the other variables or the controls on them. The result of the computer run this time was that the resource base held up, but collapse ensued again—caused this time by dangerous levels of pollution generated by the increase in industrial production. The research team continued with the computer simulations, each time putting controls in place to deal with whatever limit was encountered in the previous run. In the final simulation, big assumptions are being made about resource, food, and energy availability, and pollution and population controls. Even with all this in place, the world system collapses due to a series of problems involving land use, food availability, and pollution.

The research team drew two basic conclusions from this exercise. First, environmental problems tend to be interrelated, so 'solving' one might just mean creating another. In the environmental policy context this has led to questions around the suitability of the traditional 'departmental' or 'silo' approach to policy-making, with the environment department separate from all the others. The Club of Rome research suggests that a more 'holistic' approach is needed, and we will explore this suggestion in greater detail in the Chapter 3.

The second conclusion was that although technological solutions can prolong the period of industrial growth, the ultimate limits to that growth—represented by the finite Earth—remain. As we saw in Chapter 1, this is a big challenge to mainstream politics, in which success is largely judged by how much the economy is growing. The main criticism of the limits to growth thesis is that it underestimates the capacity of human ingenuity, especially in the form of technological advances, to solve environmental problems. In the 1990s a new approach to policy-making emerged which went by the name of 'ecological modernization'. Ecological modernizers recognized the existence of environmental problems, but argued that they could be solved without wholesale changes in our habits and practices, by the intelligent application of science and technology. Above all, they said, our production processes could be made much more efficient, creating less environmental damage for each unit of output. These initiatives went by the name of 'Factor 4' or 'Factor 10', thereby signalling the potential for four-fold or even ten-fold improvements in efficiency in regard to the trade-off between the processes of production and environmental impact.

Contemporary critics of ecological modernization argue that the best we can do is only ever to *relatively* decouple environmental impact and economic output. This means that while we can indeed reduce such impact for each unit of production, environmental impact will still go on increasing in total. For *absolute* decoupling to take place, efficiency gains would have to be made faster than growth. These critics argue that there is little evidence of this ever having happened and not much likelihood of it either.

The *Limits to Growth* report is the starting point for many of the debates that swirl around the environmental politics of the global North. We have already seen how it sets up a debate about the proper direction of travel: can mainstream politics and economics accommodate the limits challenge, or is a radical shift of direction required? Even if we can reform our way to sustainability, won't some curtailment of our freedoms be required, and won't we at the very least have to put up with inconveniences such as wind turbines in beauty spots?

The report also put population growth near the heart of environmental concern—'Malthus with a computer' was one description of its methodology and findings. This led to the criticism that the report is a thinly veiled attack on the poor and vulnerable, as expressed (for some) in the form of Garrett Hardin's 'lifeboat ethics'. Hardin argued that in resource terms the world is like a lifeboat, with room for sixty people in it, surrounded by a hundred swimmers. The lifeboat represents the rich countries and the swimmers represent poor countries. This metaphor trades on the limits to growth argument by stressing the apparently fixed quantity of resources available on the lifeboat. Hardin argued that taking all hundred swimmers on board the lifeboat would result in disaster, as there are only sufficient resources for sixty. This leaves one option it seems: leave the hundred swimmers in the water. Hardin's 'ethic' appears to deny the poor a fair share of the Earth's resources, and this extrapolation of the 'limits' thesis brought it into disrepute in some quarters.

Population growth has remained a bone of contention in environmental politics. For some it is just obvious that the more people there are, the more pressure there will be on the resource base. For others, more factors come into play. Paul Ehrlich, biologist and Professor of Population Studies, captured this more complex analysis with his formula I(mpact) = P(opulation) × A(ffluence) × T(echnology). This shows that while bare population figures are indeed important when calculating environmental impact, the level and rate of consumption (affluence), and the processes used to obtain and process resources (technology), are also crucial factors. Ehrlich's formula is often used by those who argue that small yet affluent populations are more environmentally damaging than large poorer ones.

Whose welfare?

Whatever side one is on in the 'limits' debate, one apparently unassailable assumption is that the objective of environmental policy is the welfare of human beings. And when we think of maximizing human welfare we usually think of this in terms of human beings alive today—present generation human beings. This is very much the focus of the global South environmentalism we discussed at the beginning of the chapter. (Even there, though, activists will offer other types of reason for environmental care, such as a sacred reverence for nature.) There are other possibilities beyond a concern for present day humans, though. We could broaden the 'moral community' to include, for example, future generations of human beings: we take care of the environment not only for our benefit but also for the benefit of those yet to be born. This idea is captured in the oft-quoted definition of sustainable development in the Brundtland Report, *Our Common Future*, of 1987: 'development that meets the needs of the present without compromising the ability of future generations to meet their own needs'. From this point of view it would be wrong for the present generation to respond to the threat of non-renewable resource scarcity by bingeing on those resources so as to maximize present generation welfare, leaving nothing for the future. The principles of sustainable development enjoin us to use non-renewable resources wisely and sparingly, while developing alternatives to them for use by future generations.

There is a big debate to be had, though, about just how much the present can be expected to do for the future. If it turned out that the needs of future people could only be met by sacrificing some of the *needs* of the present, would this be acceptable? Perhaps not. But what if future needs could only be met by sacrificing some of the present generation's *wants*—such as flying to New York to do the Christmas shopping? Would this be a legitimate restriction on present freedoms? Even aside from cases like this, we do tend to regard present lives as worth more than future ones (just as we tend to value lives lived closer to us—family, friends, co-nationals—than those lived further away), and this is represented in what economists call the 'discount rate'.

Formally, the discount rate is a way of calculating how much we are prepared to pay today for benefits in the future. So in the environmental context the question might be, how much is it worth to us today to avoid environmental damage (e.g., climate change) in the future? The discount rate we use is very revealing of how important we think the future is. So at a 3 per cent discount rate, we (the present generation) regard £100 ($152 or €134) of environmental damage in the year 2100 as worth about £7 ($10 or €9.5). Another way of putting this is to say that we regard the present as about fourteen times more valuable than the future—and 3 per cent is a pretty typical discount rate. Obviously, the more the discount rate tends towards zero, the more valuable we take the future to be. Debates around climate change policy—indeed any policy with implications for the medium- to long-term future—are heavily influenced by the prevailing discount rate. At a 3 per cent discount rate we can't justify spending much on climate change today, and a second objection to doing so is that future generations are usually better off than present ones, which puts them in a better position to pay for climate change mitigation and/or adaptation (of course, this assumes that effective climate change policy is a matter of spending money). From this point of view, the job of the present generation is to create the conditions to make the future richer, not to spend money on mitigating climate change.

However big or small we think the discount rate should be, or even if we think we should take no special action in regard to the interests of the future, all of the above suggests a conviction that future people do have interests, and that they should be taken into account. This clearly has implications for decisions we take today which will have an impact on the future—like whether to build nuclear power stations or not.

Moral extensionism—Factor X

At this point we can introduce two ideas which play a key role in environmental ethics—'moral extensionism', and theories of value. When we decide that the interests of future people should be weighed in the moral balance, we are *extending the moral community*. Effectively, we take the 'model' moral subject—the present generation human being—and ask what it is that makes it a moral subject. The answer might be: it is human. But because future humans are human too, what reason could we possibly have for denying them what is called 'moral considerability'? The only reason we could have for doing so is that somehow their being *future* humans disqualifies them from being moral subjects. But this would be as arbitrary as saying that the interests of women should not be weighed in the moral balance, because in addition to being human they are also female.

We can see from this that there is a 'Factor X' at work in moral extensionism—Factor X is the characteristic that makes something 'morally considerable'. In the case we have just discussed, Factor X is 'being human'. Obviously much will turn on what we think the Factor X is, and the moral community will expand and contract accordingly. We can illustrate this by looking at two contrasting Factor X accounts, from Aristotle and Jeremy Bentham, respectively. Aristotle famously asked himself what makes 'man', of all the animals, a *political* animal. The answer he gave was that man has the capacity to speak. Other animals can make noises (they have 'voice', in Aristotle's terms), but none of them can use speech to discuss what is right and wrong, just and unjust, good and evil. So for Aristotle, Factor X is 'the capacity to use speech and reason'.

In 1789, the year of the French Revolution, the utilitarian philosopher Jeremy Bentham wrote *An Introduction to the Principles of Morals and Legislation*. In a footnote to chapter xvii, in answer to his own question as to what makes a being morally considerable, he wrote, 'The question is not can they reason? Nor, can they talk? But can they suffer?' Bentham's Factor X is 'the capacity to suffer', and this widens the ethical community at a stroke—evidently the set containing beings capable of experiencing pain and pleasure (this is more generally what Bentham means by 'suffering') is much bigger than the set containing beings capable of reasoned speech. This, then, is how moral extensionism works, starting with the being which has undisputed moral considerability—the human being—identifying the characteristic it possesses that gives it such considerability, and then looking for other beings that share the characteristic.

Moral extensionism has been crucial for the animal rights movement (see Figure 3). In *Animal Liberation* (1975), the Australian philosopher Peter Singer took Bentham's insight and constructed a utilitarian ethical scheme that included non-human animals capable of experiencing pain and pleasure. A right action, for Singer, is one that contributes to the greatest good of the greatest number—*including* non-human animals capable of

3. Do all animals have rights? Or just some? How do we decide?

experiencing pleasure and pain. Similarly, the American philosopher, Tom Regan, argued in *The Case for Animal Rights* (1983) that the relevant Factor X (though he didn't use the term) is to be the 'subject-of-a-life', by which he means a being capable of having beliefs, memory, and self-consciousness, among other characteristics. The set of beings with these characteristics is bigger than the set of beings capable of reasoned speech (Aristotle) and smaller than the set that can experience pain and pleasure (Singer).

These theoretical moves have provided the foundations for a thriving animal rights/liberation movement which has made significant practical gains. Under pressure from the movement, countries have passed laws designed to improve the lives of animals in the farming industry, restrictions have been placed on the use of animals in pharmaceutical testing and the fashion/beauty industry, the use of animals in circuses has been progressively scaled back, conditions in zoos have improved, and the Dutch Party for the Animals was the first in the world to gain parliamentary seats (in 2006) with an agenda focused mainly on animal rights. By 2014 it had two members in the House of Representatives, one in the Senate, and one in the European Parliament.

Elsewhere, the idea that if humans have rights then animals similar to humans in relevant respects should have similar rights has given rise to the Great Ape Project, which argues for humanlike rights to life, liberty, and freedom from torture for chimpanzees, gorillas, and orangutans. In 2013, India banned captive dolphin facilities on the grounds that cetaceans are 'non-human persons', and in late 2014 an orangutan in Argentina called Sandra was granted a transfer from a zoo to a sanctuary for the same reasons. A 26-year-old chimpanzee called Tommy who lives alone in a shed in upstate New York was not so lucky. A court ruled in 2014 that because the chimp is not able to assume the responsibilities that go along with rights, he could not be granted legal personhood, and so his owner was not obliged to release him.

All of these arguments have been underpinned by some version or another of moral extensionism, and this introduces the second theme which plays a key role in environmental ethics: theories of value. For our purposes we can say that things can have either instrumental value or intrinsic value (or some combination of them). Instrumental value is the value something has for me when I want to get something done or pursue some goal. Intrinsic value is the value that any existing thing has, regardless of whether or not it is useful to me or anyone is there to value it.

Once we regard something as intrinsically valuable we can no longer treat it only instrumentally, without regard for its own interests. This is what lies behind campaigns to improve the lives of farm animals—beef cattle, for example. Clearly we are using them (instrumentally) for their meat, but respecting their intrinsic value might lead us to campaign against intensive cattle farming and in favour of rearing cattle outdoors on grass.

Ethics and the environment

We have spent some time talking about the ethical status of animals, and this is where moral extensionism tends to lead. But an ethic for animals is not an *environmental* ethic, and environmental politics is about more than the defence of non-human animals. There have been attempts to generate a broader environmental ethic using moral extensionism, and we will look at this when we discuss 'deep ecology'. First, though, it is important to see that caring for the environment can be justified by the instrumental value it has for human beings.

On several occasions we have referred to the environment as our 'life-support' system. This means that the environment is instrumentally valuable to us in that without it we would not be able to achieve whatever goals we set ourselves. Put differently, a healthy and functioning environment is a precondition for human welfare. This is by far the most common and widely held reason for taking care of the environment, and its strength is that it speaks to people's common sense: it just seems obvious that our wellbeing depends on a healthy environment, so we need to look after it. But this is not the only way of working up an ethic for the environment, and one key criticism of the instrumental approach leads us in another direction entirely.

The criticism is that the instrumental approach is as much a part of the problem as part of the solution. The general idea is that if we regard something as valuable only in so far as it is a means to our satisfaction, we have no reason to look after it if it doesn't have that instrumental use. It is hard to argue that every single bit of our environment is useful to us, and this means that some components of the environment are 'redundant'. So one problem with the instrumental route to an environmental ethic is that it is unlikely to be a *full* environmental ethic.

The second problem underpins the first. Imagine that we only valued other human beings because they were instrumentally useful to us. Not only would this mean that some human beings were not valuable to us (they are not all useful to us all the time), but we would also think that this was the wrong reason for valuing human beings in the first place. A proper ethic towards other human beings would not so much involve seeing them all as instrumentally useful, but of avoiding instrumentalism altogether. This is the approach taken by some environmental ethicists towards the environment.

Deep ecology

A key figure in this debate is the Norwegian philosopher, Arne Naess. In September 1972 Naess gave a lecture in Bucharest in which he distinguished between 'shallow' and 'deep' ecology. He characterized shallow ecology as a concern about 'pollution and resource depletion' for the damaging effects this might have on human life. This is, in other words, the instrumentalism we referred to above. Naess contrasted this with a 'deep' concern for the environment for its own sake. The importance of this for Naess was that care for something for its own sake affords that thing stronger protection than if it is only of instrumental value. One way of understanding this is in terms of intrinsic value, such that the environment as a whole has intrinsic value rather than just parts of it. We saw moral extensionism working, earlier, to 'share' intrinsic value between human beings and (some) non-human animals on the grounds that these animals share some Factor X with humans that confers intrinsic value on them. Is there a Factor X that could take us beyond an animal ethic towards an ethic for the environment?

Clearly, the favoured candidates of animal rights theory, such as the capacity to experience pleasure and pain, or to be a 'subject-of-a-life', will only get us so far. A common requirement for both of these is a central nervous system—something 'the environment' does not possess. An alternative favoured by environmental ethicists is 'an interest in wellbeing'. This Factor X would underpin an environmental ethic in two ways. First, it can arguably be applied to the whole of the environment, and second, it can be applied to 'wholes' like species and ecosystems, while animal rights tends to focus on individual animals (and only on a species in so far as it is a collection of animals, rather than something worth protecting in its own right). Another candidate is 'autopoesis', or the capacity for self-regeneration and self-renewal.

Anthropocentrism

An environmental ethic like this is an attempt to move away from not only instrumentalism, but also from 'anthropocentrism'. We are being anthropocentric when we arbitrarily place the interests of human beings above those of non-human nature. One way to guard against such arbitrariness is to show that non-human nature is similar to human beings in morally relevant respects—and that is what the Factor X gambit is designed to achieve.

There are a number of alternatives to anthropocentrism, but the most common are *biocentrism*, which asserts that non-human as well as human life has intrinsic value, and *ecocentrism*, which asserts that the environment of non-living things, as well as living things themselves, has intrinsic value. This means that the ecocentric finds intrinsic value in inanimate objects such as rocks and mountains—or what is sometimes called the 'abiotic' (non-living) world.

The Factor X approach to developing an environmental ethic is vulnerable to the objection that the argument is self-fulfilling. Rather than start with the human being and work outwards (moral extensionism/animal rights), it often looks as though the environmental ethicist starts with an assumption that the environment should be protected and then searches for a Factor X that will underpin the moral case for protection. For some, this dilutes the strength of moral extensionism too much, to the point at which it is no longer effective. Moral extensionism works by persuading us that a special feature possessed by humans is also possessed by other beings, so to exclude those other beings from the moral community would be inconsistent and irrational. Now take the 'interest in wellbeing' we referred to above. The problem is not so much that this isn't a characteristic shared by beings other than human beings, but that it isn't particularly *special*. It buys moral recognition at the cost of cheapening the price of recognition.

Another problem is that, ironically, the moral extensionist route to an environmental ethic may be too anthropocentric. Even if it doesn't regard the non-human world as purely an instrument for the realization of human ends, it still takes the human being to be the *measure* as well as the *source* of value.

These problems with using moral extensionism to achieve an environmental ethic have led some ecocentrics to take a different approach, one which revolves around the developing of an 'ecological consciousness' that connects the individual with the wider world. This is an expanded conception of the self which leads to an identification of the individual with all of life and the environment that sustains it. Once this identification is established, we come to see that self-realization involves working for the prospering of our surroundings too. If we understood better our condition as connected beings, it is said, we would see that harming the environment is effectively harming ourselves, and this is irrational.

Most politics is/are an answer to the question: how should we live? Or, more particularly, how should we live *together*? In two ways, environmental politics adds a new element to that question. First, the environment is an unavoidable context for both the question and the answer. No other politics foregrounds the environment in this way—indeed most of them have only come to take the environment into account under pressure from the environmental movement. The second novel contribution is that the 'together' potentially includes other living and non-living things. Most other politics only consider the relations between human beings when they ask how we are to live together. The first half of this chapter has shown how, potentially, the 'political community' is much bigger than that.

'Ecologism' as a political ideology

Yet while environmental politics brings new considerations to the table, it draws on and relates to more traditional forms of politics and political expression. One way of illustrating this is by thinking of environmental politics in terms of 'ideology'—i.e., as a set of ideas like 'socialism' or 'conservatism'. As we are thinking of it here, an ideology generally has three components: first, a critique (or sometimes an endorsement) of the way things are; second, a picture of the ideal society according to the ideology in question (which for conservatism, for example, may not be so different to the one we already have); and, third, a strategy for getting from where we are now to where the ideology would like us to be—i.e., a way of connecting the first and second components. No ideology will only have one set of answers to these questions, so it is usually more helpful to think of ideologies in plural terms—i.e., socialisms, liberalisms, nationalisms, and so on. This plurality is often reflected in putting an adjective in front of the ideology's name, as in *social* liberalism, *libertarian* socialism, *one nation* conservatism. Having said that, every ideology will have an element or elements that make it different from other ideologies—a beating heart, as it were. So we can think of ideologies and the relationships between them as a Venn diagram, illustrating their distinct and shared components.

The names of most ideologies end in -ism, and the environmental variety is no different. There are, though, two competing names and this can lead to confusion: environmentalism and ecologism. 'Environmentalism' is probably the name most people associate with environmental politics, but there have been attempts to distinguish environmentalism and ecologism on grounds similar to those introduced above. Elsewhere, I have distinguished between the two as follows:

> environmentalism argues for a managerial approach to environmental problems, secure in the belief that they can be solved without fundamental changes in present values or patterns of production and consumption

while,

> ecologism holds that a sustainable and fulfilling existence presupposes radical changes in our relationship with the non-human natural world, and in our mode of social and political life

On this account, environmentalism is less 'radical' than ecologism, and government ministers do not suddenly become political ecologists by trading in their limousines for hybrid (electric/ petrol) cars. Environmentalism is more easily incorporated into other ideologies. So we can imagine a 'liberal environmentalism' or a 'socialist environmentalism', but it is harder to imagine a liberal or a socialist *ecologism*. Why might this be? What is the beating heart of ecologism that distinguishes it from other ideologies—and from environmentalism?

The answer to these questions lies in the first half of this chapter and in Chapter 1. It is a matter of making a choice on two key issues: the first is limits to growth; and the second concerns why we should value the natural environment. It will be remembered that there were two main responses to the limits to growth idea: either that greater efficiency would overcome these apparent constraints on growth, or that the limits are real and more or less fixed. More technically, we distinguished between the *relative* and the *absolute* decoupling of growth and environmental impact. While it is widely recognized that efficiency gains can be made such that the environmental impact per unit of production can be reduced (relative decoupling), this is not the same as reducing aggregate impact (absolute decoupling). So imagine we build 100 cars at a rate of 1 unit of environmental impact per car—this makes 100 units of environmental impact. Imagine, now, that we improve our environmental efficiency by 10 per cent per car. This will allow us to build 110 cars for the same impact as 100 cars when we were operating in a less efficient way. But if we build 111 cars or more, we will still be increasing our aggregate environmental impact despite our efficiency gains. In rough-and-ready terms we might say that those who are satisfied with relative decoupling are environmentalists, while those who see the challenge as one of organizing society around the impossibility of absolute decoupling are political ecologists (we use this term rather than simply 'ecologists' to distinguish the politics from the science).

In terms of other ideologies, relative decoupling is less of a challenge to their core positions than is absolute decoupling in that it does not call growth, as such, into question. Other modern ideologies take economic growth as an objective for society for granted—indeed they measure the success of a society in terms of such growth: is gross domestic product (GDP) increasing or decreasing? In this sense, adopting concerns around absolute decoupling would amount to questioning a core—if often unstated—belief at the heart of those ideologies. This, then, is one of the central beliefs of the ideology of ecologism: that aggregate growth must be reduced, and that this is very unlikely to be achieved by efficiency gains alone.

The other core belief turns on the question of why (if at all) we should value the non-human natural world. Earlier we saw that there are two broad approaches to this: we can value it either instrumentally or intrinsically. In other words, we can value it because it is a means to human ends, or we can value it as an end in itself. Once the issue is drawn to one's attention, it seems commonsensical to value nature instrumentally, if only because that enhances the chances of human flourishing—and even survival. In regard to other ideologies, there is absolutely no incompatibility between their core beliefs and an instrumental valuing of nature. In fact we might say that other ideologies ought actively to incorporate this valuing of nature in their systems, as a functioning environment is a precondition for whatever world they would like to see—conservative, liberal, socialist, or nationalist.

Valuing non-human nature *intrinsically* is much trickier for these other ideologies, though. Their basic *raison d'être* is the maximization of human welfare, and non-human nature is only valuable in so far as it contributes to human welfare. Those who would value nature intrinsically are calling this objective into question, at least as an overriding principle. At the very least they will question the assumption that human *wants* should be satisfied at the expense of non-human *needs*. This demand that the needs of non-human nature be taken into account for their own sake is too disruptive of the settled assumptions of other ideologies for them to accept it. It is this, together with the idea that aggregate growth must be reduced, that form the core beliefs of what we are calling ecologism.

Other ideologies—conservatism

Having said that, the Venn diagram point we made earlier suggests that there will be points of overlap between ecologism and other ideologies. Here we will look at conservatism, liberalism, socialism, and feminism (the choice is difficult—anarchism, for instance, is also an interesting comparator). There is obviously a common etymological root between conservation and conservatism, so it should not surprise us to find some similarities between conservatism and ecologism. The conservative view of what *should* be done is very much underpinned by considerations of what *can* be done, and the limits to growth thesis—which is, as we have seen, so important to ecologism—is very much a reminder that we can't do everything we might imagine doing. Conservatives urge caution, and in similar vein political ecologists urge *pre*caution. The precautionary principle is a key element in environmental policy-making, and it states that if there is any risk of harm to the environment by adopting a certain policy, then the burden of proof that it is not harmful falls on those who wish to pursue the policy. We might regard this as a conservative approach to risk, the alternative to which is to go ahead with the policy and clean up afterwards (if necessary and if possible).

Earlier in this chapter, we noted that green thinking expands the moral community by taking account of the interests of future humans as well as present ones. Of all contemporary ideologies, the one that comes closest to sharing this view is conservatism. It was Edmund Burke, the so-called 'father of English conservatism', who said that society was a 'partnership not only between those who are living, but between those who are living, those who are dead, and those who are to be born'. There is a potentially significant difference in emphasis in that conservatives tend to look to the past, while—as we have seen on a number of occasions—the environmental focus is often on the future. Conservatism is interested in the conserving and preserving of the past, while ecologism is interested in conserving and preserving for the future. Despite this, 'intergenerationalism'—a concern for the relationship between generations and what they might owe each other—is unique to conservatism and ecologism in political thought.

This picture of conservatism painted here will not be recognized by someone brought up with the liberal 'conservatism' of the last forty years or so. This is a form of small state, free-market liberalism in which economic decisions are left to the market, and the common good (what is good for all of us, as a society) is produced by all of us pursuing our self-interest. Any attempt by the state to steer society in a given direction will inevitably amount to a restriction on the freedom of individuals to pursue their self-interest, and will also result in bad ('sub-optimal') decisions anyway; the state, it is said, has proved itself incapable of backing (economic) winners—only the market can. Free-marketeers argue that one of the fundamental principles of the market—private property—is the best instrument we have for sustainability, on the grounds that private property is better looked after than property held in common. Sceptics will respond that there are some excellent examples of sustainably managed property held in common, such as Swedish forests, and that the private property-owner might calculate that he or she would be better off selling the forest and turning a profit (for example), rather than looking after it for the sake of its human and non-human inhabitants and for the future.

Liberalism

This economic liberalism has changed the face of conservatism, but it is not the only liberalism there is. Our discussion of the potential inclusion of some animals in the moral community was an implicit recognition of the importance of another strand of liberalism in this aspect of environmental thinking. This is because 'rights'—including animal rights—are a fundamentally liberal idea. What is revolutionary about rights is that they are like a passport to a certain kind of treatment and respect that cannot be taken away—in technical terms, they are 'inalienable'. They amount to a powerful claim, and it is much better to be a possessor of rights than not. Beneficiaries of environmental-rights talk in our context include present generations of humans (where the idea of a right to a clean and healthy environment has gained traction—even to the point of being included in some countries' constitutions), future generations of humans (as we have seen on a number of occasions), and some non-human animals. Recognizing these rights in practice is another matter altogether, of course, but such is their authority in political discourse that they throw a spotlight of legitimacy on to anyone or anything that can plausibly lay claim to possessing them. On a broader canvas, it is worth remembering that it was a liberal— John Stuart Mill—who described, in his *Principles of Political Economy*, the 'stationary state' society in terms that many greens would endorse:

> there [is not] much satisfaction in contemplating the world with nothing left to the spontaneous activity of nature... If the earth must lose that great portion of its pleasantness—which it owes to things that the unlimited increase of wealth and population would extirpate from it for the mere purpose of enabling it to support a larger, but not a better or a happier population—I sincerely hope, for the sake of posterity, that we humans will be content to be stationary, long before necessity compels us to it.

In other regards, though, liberalism has a more problematic relationship with environmental politics—and especially with ecologism as we described it above. First, liberalism has at its heart a concern for liberty, generally understood as the freedom to do what one wants, consistent with other people's similar freedoms. Ecological thinking might be regarded as going against the liberal grain in this respect, in two ways.

First, the requirement to keep within the limits of a finite Earth might be read as a series of prohibitions on production, consumption, and mobility. It is not that these restrictions can't be justified in liberal terms, since liberals often operate a 'harm principle' which says that my freedoms end where harm to others begins. It is possible to think of overconsumption as doing harm, in the sense of encroaching on others' 'ecological space', and in this sense, liberal justifications of sustainability-related restrictions are possible. But these restrictions will never come naturally to the liberal sensibility, partly because liberals tend to make an important distinction between preferences (what they want to do) and interests (what it is in their interest to do). More particularly, liberals will say that their preferences *are* their interests, and they will resist the idea that anyone could know their interests better than they can. But this, of course, is what greens will often claim—they are in the business of 'enlightening' us as to the true state of things: our preference (to take one long-haul foreign holiday every year) may not be in our best interests (a stable climate).

Relatedly, liberals believe that we should be free to choose our own moral code, and that it is not the job of politics—and far less the state—to tell us what the contours of the 'good life' should be. This is why, while liberals are happy for people to practise whatever religion they wish, they are opposed to the state deciding for us which religion we should follow. Think of a roundabout, with various exits. The rules of the roundabout ensure that the cars are kept apart, and the drivers may take any exit they wish. The rules of the roundabout represent the rules of society, preventing people from harming each other as they go about satisfying their preferences, and the exits represent the various versions of the good life that people choose to pursue. In theory, in a liberal society citizens are free to take any exit they wish, and to create new ones, as long as they respect similar freedoms of other citizens and don't cause them harm. The potential conflict with green thinking is that from a sustainability point of view not all exits from the roundabout will be regarded as legitimate or desirable: the need to keep production and consumption within the limits of a finite planet, and the injunction to recognize the intrinsic value of non-human nature, both act as constraints on our plans for life, and could well close off some types of exit from the roundabout. To this degree, ecologism might be regarded as 'non-liberal'.

Socialism

Historically, liberalism has had two views of non-human nature, one drawing on John Locke, who saw nature as a storehouse for human benefit, and one with a more benign view, represented by Bentham's 'sentience' criterion for moral considerability, and Mill's 'stationary state' society. Mill's *Principles of Political Economy*, where he described the stationary state society, was published in 1848—the same year as Karl Marx's *The Communist Manifesto*. Although they are a long way apart in many respects, what Locke and Marx have in common—and where they part company with Mill—is the belief that human progress consists in dominating nature and putting it to work for our benefit alone. Just as 'a view from nature' shows that there are two strands of liberalism, the same is true of socialism. One wing is represented by Marx and his heirs, promoting a productivist socialism, and the other, represented by so-called utopian socialists such as William Morris, offers a less productivist, more decentralized form of socialism.

Unsurprisingly, it is the latter type of socialism with which political ecologists have more in common, not least because Morris and his colleagues tended to view 'industrialism' rather than capitalism as the source of humanity's ills. This is consistent with the analysis of many contemporary political ecologists who argue that as far as the key issue of growth is concerned, there is little difference between mainstream socialism and mainstream capitalism—the objective of both is to grow the economy as fast as possible. Marx felt that capitalism was a brake on productivity, and that is why he argued it needed to be overthrown. On the other hand, capitalists argue against socialism on the grounds that productivity is best achieved by leaving the market to its own devices, and socialism brings with it too much state intervention in the market. What is common to them both, though, is the maximizing of production and growth.

Ecologism and socialism share a concern for the connected ideas of equality and justice. Much of ecologism's determination to extend ethical concern to the environment is animated by the idea that equality should apply 'beyond the human'. The same goes for justice. For socialism, justice is about universal recognition of all as participants in creating society's common wealth, and about the fair shares that everyone deserves as a result of this common endeavour. There are evident echoes of this in ecologism, where the non-human environment is regarded as a partner in, and contributor to, whatever prosperity we may enjoy, and therefore deserving of recognition, care, and justice. Justice is also clearly at the heart of the 'environmentalism of the poor' to which we have referred on several occasions. Here it plays two roles. First, this version of environmental politics sees environmental problems as caused by injustice which forces the disadvantaged to degrade their environment. And, second, environmental 'bads' (such as landfills) are disproportionately—and unjustly—located in poor communities.

From this brief survey of three ideologies in relation to ecologism—conservatism, liberalism, and socialism—we can see that the interesting fault lines are less between ecologism and these ideologies and more the ones we find *within* these ideologies. In each case there is a strand that calls into question the idea that wellbeing is necessarily linked with economic growth; and a simultaneous sense that we lose something through our progressive alienation from the non-human natural world. In the Venn diagram illustrating the relationship between ecologism and other ideologies, the overlap areas will be bigger in relation to these 'subordinate' streams than their mainstream, more dominant, partners.

Feminism

One final ideology has played an especially significant role in the development of environmental politics—feminism. Just as there are many liberalisms and socialisms, though, so there are many feminisms, and one of these has been especially influential. Recall the remark we have just made: the sense that we lose something by being so distanced from nature. This prompts the question: how do we close that distance? One type of feminism—often called 'difference' feminism—offers a possible answer. As the name suggests, difference feminists argue that men and women are fundamentally different, and one of the ways they are different is that women are said to be 'closer to nature'. This is because of women's key role in 'reproducing life', either as birth-givers or—as is still the case in most of the world—as those who shoulder much of the work of sustaining life. The argument goes that this closeness to nature puts women in the vanguard as far as reconfiguring our relationship with the natural world is concerned.

Even if this analysis is correct, though, some feminists see it as involving a high-risk strategy for women. This is because one of the reasons given to legitimate women's subordination in the past was, precisely, their supposed closeness to nature. In a world in which nature is regarded as wild, unpredictable, irrational, and a realm of passion, and in a world in which these characteristics are regarded as incompatible with the practices of civilization, any group wanting to take part in these practices would do well to resist those characteristics. An alternative, of course, is to revalue those characteristics, and to view passion and wildness more positively. If this were the case, then groups associated with passion and wildness would be better regarded. The danger, of course, is that if this revaluation doesn't take place, women are left where they were before—subordinate to men.

This problem has led some feminists to argue that it is not a question of aligning one or the other gender with 'nature', but of refusing the nature/culture and man/woman dualisms in the first place. This is a matter of recognizing that women are fully human and simultaneously acknowledging that human identity is continuous with nature rather than somehow different from it. This is a kind of reconfigured humanism. From an environmental point of view, humanism can be problematic if it simply amounts to a reassertion of the sway of humanity over nature. In contrast, this version would be a win-win for both women and nature: women would no longer be battling for acceptance, and nature would benefit from being regarded as on a continuum with humanity.

This chapter has been about some of the key ideas that drive environmental politics, but in politics there is no point in having ideas unless there is some way of putting them into practice. Chapter 3 is about the 'machinery' of environmental politics—the movement that nurtures and expresses the politics; the parties that are the electoral vehicles for getting the politics into the system; and the array of policy instruments that are available for putting society on a more sustainable footing.

Chapter 3
Movements, parties, policies

The environmental movement

There is no definition of the 'environmental movement' that is sufficiently authoritative for us to be able to say exactly who or what is in it. It has been defined by Christopher Rootes and Robert Brulle as,

> networks of informal interactions that may include, as well as individuals and groups who have no organisational affiliation, organisations of varying degrees of formality (including even political parties, especially Green parties) that are engaged in collective action motivated by shared identity of concern about environmental issues. Such networks are generally loose and uninstitutionalised, but the forms of action and degree of integration vary. Environmental movements are, however, identical neither with organisations nor with episodes of protest. It is only when organisations (and other, usually less formally organised actors) are networked and engaged in collective action, whether or not it involves protest, that an environmental movement exists.

This account includes political parties within the definition of the environmental movement, but here we will be treating them separately, for two reasons. First, because parties participate in politics in a very specific way—they seek election. Organizations that form part of the environmental movement don't do this. Second, political parties are expected to offer policies across the whole range of issues, including defence, education, welfare, and so on. Environmental movement organizations tend to focus on single issues, so while Compassion in World Farming will lobby on behalf of farm animals, it will not have policies for defence and education. A Green political party will have policies for animal welfare *and* for defence and education.

Second, there are debates about what sort of organization can be counted as part of the environmental movement. There are some obvious candidates such as Greenpeace and Friends of the Earth, the Sierra Club in the USA, the Goa Foundation in India, and the Australian Rainforest Conservation Society. But then there is the National Trust in the UK which is normally associated with the conservation of historic buildings. This preoccupation with the *built* environment might rule it out of membership of the environmental movement if we take this to be about the *natural* environment. The National Trust, though, is also responsible for the protection of coastlines, forests, farmland, moorland, and nature reserves. Does this make the National Trust a member of the environmental movement after all?

The question is complicated further by the fact that the 'movement' comprises campaigns as well as organizations (see Figure 4), and often the character of these campaigns can shift from obviously environmental to less so, and back again. This is particularly true of campaigns in the majority world, or the global South, and this is largely because, as we have seen, environmental issues and questions of livelihood are often intimately bound up there. An example is the Movement for the Survival of the Ogoni People in Nigeria (MOSOP). This movement may not sound 'environmental'—until we see that the welfare of the Ogoni people is tied up with the activities of the Shell oil corporation, which has been accused of inflicting massive environmental damage on the Niger Delta through oil extraction and dumping.

4. People's Climate March, New York, September 2014.

These difficulties over definition make authoritative estimates of the membership of the 'environmental movement' hard to come by. One recent (2013) survey of 139 organizations in the UK put the aggregate membership at 4.5 million—or roughly 10 per cent of the potential population. Others have put it as high as 20 per cent, with anything between 7 per cent and 16 per cent for other countries such as Australia and the USA. In India there are over sixty environmental NGOs in the US Environmental Directories list. These are impressive numbers in the political context, especially when set against membership of political parties. In the UK, less than 1 per cent of the population belongs to a political party, while in Australia there are more people on the waiting list for membership of Melbourne Cricket Club then there are members of all the political parties combined.

The history of the environmental movement

This amounts to a considerable social and political resource, and it has been built up over more than a hundred years. The development of the environmental movement is generally reckoned to have taken place in two phases. The first began in the 19th century with the founding of protection and conservation organizations such as the Royal Society for the Protection of Birds in the UK (1889), and the Sierra Club in the USA (1892). Around this period and beyond, national parks were founded across much of the world, from Yellowstone Park (USA, 1834) to Ordesa y Monte Perdido Park in Aragón (Spain, 1918), Halley's National Park in Uttarakhand (India, 1932), and the Peak District (UK, 1951). This is also the time when various back-to-the-land movements were founded, especially in Northern Europe, which have had an enduring influence on the contemporary environmental movement, especially in the guise of so-called 'intentional communities'—i.e., small communities which prefigure a sustainable future by living it now. There was a growing belief in the regenerative power of contact with the land, especially for those deprived of it, so the Woodcraft Folk—for example—was founded in south London in 1924–5, with the intention of giving working-class children experience of the outdoors. The Woodcraft Folk (still in existence) was itself a secession from the Kibbo Kift Kin, founded in opposition to the increasingly militaristic tendencies of the scout movement in the aftermath of World War I. The Kin aimed to establish a counter-society based on socialist and pacifist principles, but like many radical movements and people of this period it was imbued with a sense of the importance of nature as a symbol of nationhood. Some will say that this is at odds with the simultaneously more localized and globalized relationship to nature of the contemporary environmental movement. This contemporary attitude is summed up in the popular slogan 'think global, act local'.

The second phase of the development of the environmental movement began in the 1960s, as one of the so-called 'new social movements'. The word 'new' is designed to distinguish these movements from older ones rooted in the context of the struggle between capital and labour—the labour movement of the trade unions, for example. New social movements tend to work beyond the spectrum of the traditional parties, they work in the sphere of civil society (the sphere that lies between the state and the market, sometimes called the third sector), they focus on issues of diversity as much as on equality, and they tend to have decentralized forms of organization. In the environmental context, they signalled a move beyond the conservation and preservation focus of the first phase, towards campaigning on 'end-of-pipe' issues such as toxic waste, technologies such as nuclear power, and—more recently—genetically modified organisms.

Explaining the environmental movement

The social theorist Ronald Inglehart claimed that these new movements were a result of changes in the values of people in industrialized countries whose immediate material needs had been satisfied, and whose aspirations now lay in meeting less material needs. Linked to a decline in the manufacturing industries and a rise in the service industries, Inglehart called this a 'silent revolution', with

> the basic value priorities of Western publics...shifting from a Materialist emphasis towards a Postmaterialist one—from giving top priority to physical sustenance and safety towards heavier emphasis on belonging, self-expression and the quality of life.

Inglehart's thesis has many supporters, and it does reflect the tendency of the environmental movement to attract an above average number of people form the public service sector, and with higher education degrees. But it has been criticized on three main grounds. First, his range of criteria for assessing value change is rather narrow and—especially important from our point of view—it contains no specifically environmental criterion. Second, 'old' concerns of equality and fair and universal access to (environmental) goods and services are very much present in environmental movement campaigns for environmental justice, such as those pursued by Friends of the Earth. Third, it is a mistake to think of environmental issues as 'post-material' anyway. On several occasions already we have seen the environment referred to as a 'life-support system'—a very material representation of the planet we live on, and a clear reference to it as a satisfier of basic needs. This makes Inglehart's thesis even less helpful in explaining environmental movements in the global South where they are intimately bound up with the very practical and material business of campaigning for the conditions for sustainable and equitable livelihoods. Overall, Inglehart's thesis draws useful attention to key sociological features of aspects of the environmental movement in the global North, but it is less helpful in explaining activism in the global South, and in the worldwide movement for environmental justice.

Categorizing the environmental movement

However we define the environmental movement, one striking feature of it is its variety. An influential way of dealing with this diversity is to categorize organizations in terms of the types of resources they draw upon, and the way they try to influence the political process. Mario Diani and Paolo Donati offer this framework:

	Conventional pressure	**Disruption**
Professional resources	Public interest lobby	Professional protest organization
Participatory resources	Participatory pressure group	Participatory protest organization

Source: Diani and Donati: 16

Public interest groups tend to be large, mass-membership organizations which rely on the provision of information to politicians and civil servants for their political effectiveness. The membership's principal role is to pay the annual subscriptions that fund the organization's salaries, overheads, and campaigns. Examples of public interest groups are the National Wildlife

Federation and the Sierra Club in the USA, the Woodland Trust in the UK, and the Royal Forest and Bird Protection Society of New Zealand. Professional protest organizations share the characteristic of a relatively passive membership with the public interest groups, but they adopt more confrontational tactics, aiming less to influence policy-makers directly, and more to bring issues to the public's attention and thereby increase pressure for change. Greenpeace is a good example of a professional protest organization, at least in its origins. It is especially well known for its audacious actions, and for its famous *Rainbow Warrior* ship, sunk by French agents in Auckland Harbour in 1985 when it was on the way to protest against a French nuclear test in Moruroa. More recent high-profile actions include protesting against Russian drilling for oil in the Pechora Sea in 2013, which resulted in the arrest—and subsequent release—of thirty activists for 'piracy', and a (successful) 2014 campaign to stop Lego carrying Shell's logo on its figures.

Participatory protest groups tend to be small, relying on dedicated members, many of whom are also activists. Sometimes these groups are short-lived, organized around a particular action in a particular place, and dissolving once the action is completed. A UK example is the Dongas road protest group, formed to resist the expansion of the M3 motorway around Twyford Down in the south of England. A self-styled 'tribe', the Dongas were aggressively evicted from Twyford in 1992, and then moved on to other roads protests before wandering semi-nomadically around south-west England for the rest of the decade. Other participatory protest groups have a structure an organization and a purpose that enable them to operate over a long period of time. The Sea Shepherd Conservation Society, for example, was founded in the late 1970s (by Greenpeace ex-board member Paul Watson who was frustrated at what he saw as Greenpeace's ineffectiveness) with the aim of taking direct action against whaling ships around the world—and it still sails the seas today. It is a participatory group, run by volunteers and a small number of paid staff, and it is deliberately kept small to keep overheads low and to help ensure that funds are spent on the frontline rather than on backroom staff and operations.

Of the four 'types' of organization present in Diani and Donati's framework, participatory pressure groups are the least common. This is because effective lobbying demands a degree of persistence, expertise, and rapid decision-making that sits uneasily with regular participation by a large membership. Most participatory pressure groups operate with one foot in either the public interest lobby or the participatory protest category—or both. An example is 350.org, founded by the Canadian author and activist, Bill McKibben, and named after the 'safe' concentration of CO_2 in the atmosphere (350 parts per million). The pressure group 350.org is renowned for its high-quality evidence base (used by others for formal lobbying), but the organization's resources are mostly devoted to building a global climate movement and co-ordinating mass public actions, such as the People's Climate March in New York City in September 2014. This puts it firmly in the participatory protest category.

As environmental politics has become more and more a fixed and accepted feature of the political landscape, groups have tended to gravitate towards more conventional ways of influencing the political process. This is partly because the policy community is more primed to 'hear' environmental groups than it was in the past due to the increased salience of environmental politics, but also because once that trend towards conventionality has begun, groups have a vested interest in keeping it going due to the time, money, and other resources already committed to the process. A recent survey of environmental groups in the UK revealed that many of them felt that they needed to develop policy expertise grounded in evidence-based research—the classic tools in the lobbyist's toolbox.

While the conventional/disruptive/professional/participatory matrix is the basis for a helpful typology, there are other ways of distinguishing environmental groups. Another characteristic is how long the group lasts. As a general rule, local 'Not In My Back Yard' (nimby) actions, around roads or test-drilling for 'fracking', for example, tend to be relatively short-lived. The more the 'local' protest has a regional, national, or even international salience, as in rainforest protection in Latin America or dam protests in India, the more embedded and institutionalized the protest becomes. Some organizations have been around for a very long time indeed. Among what we are calling professional protest organizations, Friends of the Earth was founded in 1969 and Greenpeace in 1971, while the US public interest organization, the Sierra Club, was founded in 1892. In general, we find that the founding of the longest-lived protest organizations (coming up to fifty years old) coincided with the beginning of the second phase of the environmental movement, with the more traditional lobbying groups having a longer history—sometimes stretching back into the 19th century. As we have seen, there has been a tendency for some of the second-wave protest groups to gravitate towards lobbying as a way of influencing the political process, leaving room for more ephemeral groups to pick up the protest baton.

There are further faultlines between environmental groups in the 'protest' category—i.e., in the 'disruption' column in Diani and Donati's framework. In the first place, a protest can be legal or illegal. So a march against climate change which has been cleared with the authorities might be regarded as a legal protest, while an attempt to disrupt a badger cull by entering culling areas to prevent badgers being shot (as in the UK in 2013–14) would be an illegal protest. There is a further division in the 'illegal' category, between violent and non-violent illegal protest. Non-violent illegal protest includes 'sit-ins', occupations, and blockades. These forms of passive resistance are often regarded as taking the moral high ground, and they draw on the practice and experiences of the civil rights movement in the USA, and on Mahatma Gandhi's Satyagraha ('truth force') movement which was instrumental in ending British occupation of India.

Violent protest can be directed against people or property or both, and groups that carry out these types of action are often classed as terrorists by their governments. The animal rights movement is often associated with violent direct action, and while obviously not all animal rights supporters condone violence, let alone carry it out, the Animal Liberation Front (ALF) (for example), has garnered a reputation for impacting the political process through the use of violence. Founded in 1976 in the UK and around 1979 in the USA, the ALF is resolutely opposed to violence against people, but many of its actions have involved the destruction of laboratories, pens, and holding facilities.

A violent protest group with a broader environmental remit is Earth First! (always with the '!'), founded in the USA in 1980 and then spreading to other countries throughout the world, principally but not exclusively in the global North. Both the objectives and the methods of Earth First! are radical, and the group advocates various forms of direct action including 'monkeywrenching' and 'tree-spiking' in the pursuit of the defence of wilderness (see Figure 5). ('Monkeywrenching', or the disabling of environmentally damaging machinery, installations, or activities comes from Edward Abbey's *The Monkey Wrench Gang*, a fictional account of a band of renegades bent on destroying the Glen Canyon Dam in Northern Arizona.) Just as professional protest organizations can become institutionalized and move from protesting to lobbying, so violent environmental groups can abandon violence and embrace peaceful—but still illegal—protest. In 1992, Earth First! ceased explicitly to advocate violent direct action, and this spawned the still-active Earth Liberation Front, comprising ex-Earth-First!ers who wanted to continue to pursue the path of criminal damage.

There is one final form of environmental action that does not fit into Diani and Donati's schema, but which we should nevertheless consider to be part of the environmental movement. These are 'intentional' communities which aim to prefigure the sustainable

5. **Direct action: Earth First! anti-logging activist, California, 1993.**

society by living it today. Members of environmental intentional communities live low-impact lifestyles, often growing as much of their own food as they can, and sharing tasks and decision-making. Examples include the Kerala Commune in Palakkad (India), the Findhorn Foundation (Scotland), Twin Oaks (USA), Crystal Waters (Australia), and Otamatea Eco Village (New Zealand).

Intentional communities aim to influence the wider world through example—by practising what they preach. In terms of strategy they therefore work at the opposite end of the spectrum from professional lobby organizations—just about as far away from the corridors of power as it is possible to be. They often have outreach activities, including running educational courses both in the community and outside it, on permaculture, community-building, and the small-scale 'circular economy'. Some of them take on short-term volunteers and paying guests.

A quite recent version of prefigurative environmental politics goes by the name of the Transition Town movement. The Transition movement—largely an affluent world initiative—began in the English town of Totnes in 2006, as a response to the 'peak oil' phenomenon. 'Peak oil' refers to the moment at which maximum petroleum production is reached, at which point—given that oil is a finite resource—production will go into decline. The Transition movement is therefore an attempt to create 'resilience' in the face of what Transitioners regard as an inevitable energy shock and the instability it will bring in its train. 'Energy descent' is a common phrase in Transition theory and practice, and Transitioners promote local renewable energy and food initiatives, organize education events, and develop community-based solutions to the challenge of provisioning basic needs under conditions of scarcity. There are now around 500 'official' (initiatives have to fulfil a set of criteria) Transition Town initiatives in over thirty-five countries. Not all environmentalists embrace the necessity or desirability of the Transitioners' low energy future—UK environmentalists such as Mark Lynas and George Monbiot argue for the benefits of nuclear power, in large part because of its relatively climate-friendly nature as a source of energy.

It is hard to judge the impact of intentional communities on environmental/sustainability change, but one thing they do illustrate is the breadth of the environmental movement, ranging from professional lobbyists to communards, from peaceful resistance to violent direct action, and from short-term local struggles to long-term international campaigns. If we include Green political parties as part of the environmental movement, as many scholars do, then the movement becomes broader still. It is to these parties we now turn.

Green parties

Green parties have become a feature of many political systems over the past thirty years, and there are now about eighty countries around the world with parties promoting Green policies. As we saw in Chapter 1, the first recognizably Green party is generally reckoned to have been founded in 1972 in Tasmania, Australia, on the back of (unsuccessful) opposition to a dam on Lake Peddler, as the United Tasmania Group (UTG). Given that this was a state rather than a national party, the accolade of 'first Green party, sometimes goes to New Zealand, where the Values Party was founded just two months after the UTG. The first major electoral breakthrough came in 1983 when the West German Green party scored 5.6 per cent of the vote and, due to a favourable proportional representation electoral system, gained twenty-eight seats in the Federal Parliament. Since then, steady progress has been made through the political systems of a number of countries, to the point where the Greens have been junior coalition partners in governments in Germany, Sweden, Denmark, Italy, Ireland, the Czech Republic, France, and Finland. In ministerial terms the high-water mark was German Green Joschka Fischer's tenure as Vice Chancellor and Foreign Minister between 1998 and 2005 (Fischer came in for considerable criticism from his supporters and electors when he authorized the bombing of Serbia in the late 1990s). As the right hand side of Table 1 shows, the Green party story is generally one of increasing electoral success, but this aggregate story both hides some failures and tells us nothing about why some Green parties seem to be more consistently successful than others—or why some parties, like Aotearoa New Zealand, gain quite sudden success. Nor does it tell us anything about how

Table 1. The Green party story

Country	Most recent national election			Past performance (% of national vote)			
	Date	% of vote	Seats	1980s	1990s	2000s	
Australia	2013	8.7	1	-	1.9	8.0	
Austria	2013	12.4	24	4.8	6.0	10.9	
Belgium*	2014	8.6	12	5.9	10.9	5.5	
Canada	2011	3.9	1	-	-	4.9	
Czech Republic	2013	3.2	0	-	4.1	3.8	
Denmark**	2015	4.2	7	12.5	9.0	7.8	
Finland***	2015	8.5	15	2.8	6.9	8.1	
France†	2012	5.5	17	1.1	7.2	4.4	

Germany	2013	8.4	63	5.1	6.3	9.0
Netherlands††	2012	2.3	4	-	5.0	5.1
New Zealand/Aotearoa	2014	10.7	14	-	6.1	8.2
Norway	2013	2.8	1	0.4	0.2	1.5
Sweden	2014	6.9	25	2.9	4.3	6.0
Switzerland	2011	8.4	15	7.1	5.5	8.5
England and Wales	2015	3.8	1	0.3	0.5	1.6

Notes: Not all countries have 'Green' parties, simply called. The major exceptions in this table are* Ecolo and Agalev/Groen;** Socialist People's Party;*** Green League;† Europe Ecologie—Les Verts;†† Green Left.

Green parties have evolved during their 'long march through the institutions'.

In relation to this last question, our discussion of organizations in the environmental movement revealed a general tendency towards professionalization, and towards research- and evidence-based lobbying as close to the centre of power as possible. Something similar has happened to Green parties as they have made a succession of organizational and policy compromises consistent with the perceived demands of working within parliamentary systems. In its early days the German Green party, for example, called itself an 'anti-party party', to signal its programmatic and organizational distance from the politics-as-usual it was aiming to challenge. Its four founding principles were social justice, ecological wisdom, grassroots democracy, and non-violence. Organizational innovations included enforced job rotation, including that of MPs, so that no MP served more than two years of any four-year electoral cycle; no single leader; no coalitions; and using the party conference as the policy-making body. Any one of these would have been a challenge to mainstream politics, but in combination they put the German Greens on a collision course with the political system so that something had to give.

The rotation principle in particular put Greens at a disadvantage because MPs found themselves out of the Bundestag just as they had got used to its ways of working. Likewise, the 'no coalition' rule limited the Greens' potential political influence. All this led to an internal battle between the 'fundis' and the 'realos' (the fundamentalists and the realists)—a battle that the realists eventually won. Many Green parties have gone through a similar evolution as their founding principles have clashed with the demands of the parliamentary system. Thus increased influence has been bought at the cost of a dilution of programmatic and organizational principles, and the question is whether on balance this has taken us closer—or left us further away from—a more just and sustainable society.

Have Green parties made a difference?

This is a difficult question to answer, not least because it is hard to isolate the effect that Green parties as opposed to other influences have had on environment and sustainability policy. At one end of the spectrum of possibilities, any advances that have been made would have happened without Green parties. At the other end, these advances are due to Green parties and no-one else. Inevitably, the truth lies somewhere in the middle. What is incontrovertible is that Greens have influenced other political parties, and most of them now have a section on 'the environment' in their manifestos and party programmes. This is a direct result of electoral competition, and it applies mostly to left-of-centre parties where competition with Greens for political space is most acute—although centre-right parties, such as the UK's Conservative Party, have also been known to paint green stripes in their blue flags as a sign of 'modernization'. Some have argued that the German Green party's roots in the anti-nuclear movement and its consistent anti-nuclear sentiment have been a key factor in Germany's phasing out of nuclear power—though others will say that this was more due to contingent events such as the Fukushima nuclear power plant disaster in Japan in March 2011.

Overall it is probably fair to say that pressure from the environmental movement—including Green parties—has pushed mainstream politics into an acceptance of ecological modernization as we described it in Chapter 2. That is, an understanding that 'the environment' is the unavoidable context for politics and economics, and that we need to look after it more effectively and use it more efficiently. It is also true to say that in periods of stress, such as the economic crisis of 2008 to the present, these objectives come to be treated as a luxury extra. David Cameron, the UK Prime Minister, who made much of his green credentials in advance of the General Election of 2010, was heard to talk in 2013 of 'all that green crap' in reference to environmental obligations apparently driving up household energy bills.

How can we explain the generally increasing success of Green parties, and the way in which some parties seem to be consistently more successful than others? At the macro level we could refer back to Ronald Inglehart's 'silent revolution'—the idea of a shift from materialist to post-materialist values. The steady electoral gains made by Green parties are consistent with the idea that increasing numbers of people have their material needs met and so turn to parties with a more post-material message. One problem with this idea is that it is wrong to see environmental politics as post-materialist in the first place. But Inglehart's thesis would also suggest a decline in Green party votes when people's material wellbeing is threatened—during the recent widespread economic crisis for example. One report found that by the end of 2010, one in six households in Europe was struggling to find enough money to live on. Contrary to this expectation, though, twelve of the countries in our table experienced a rise in their post-2008 (post-crash) vote, compared with four seeing a decline. On the other hand, Inglehart's socialization hypothesis suggests that it is the economic conditions prevailing in one's pre-adult years that count, so the effects of the 2008 economic crash on support for Green parties may not be clear for some time yet.

Similarly, Inglehart's thesis could be taken to imply a 'cohort effect', whereby those who were attracted to the new politics of the 1960s and 1970s are now at the older end of the electorate. This would suggest an increasingly older prolife for Green activists and voters, but compared to other parties, the Greens attract on average a younger (and more female and better-educated) section of the electorate. Overall, while Inglehart's thesis has some explanatory power as far as the increasing Green vote is concerned, the following factors (or a combination of them) work best at the macro level: an increased salience of environmental issues; a broadening of the appeal of Green parties beyond their 'environmental' heartlands to include social justice issues; and Green parties as a repository for a 'protest vote' against mainstream politics and politicians.

Why are some Green parties more successful than others?

As far as explaining the differing fortunes of Green parties is concerned, political scientists often use the idea of 'political opportunity structures'—that is to say, the way in which political systems themselves constitute a series of opportunities (and obstacles) for political parties. Some systems are more helpful to small parties than others (Green parties usually are small parties)—the 'structure' provides more 'opportunity'. The most important element in the structure is the electoral system; and the main determining factor is whether the electoral system is proportional or not. A proportional system awards seats in proportion to the number of votes cast for each party, usually subject to a minimum threshold (say, 5 per cent). In contrast, a majoritarian system awards seats to the party that wins a majority of votes in a given constituency. All other votes in that constituency effectively count for nothing.

By way of illustration, Germany has a proportional electoral system, while the UK has a majoritarian (or 'first past the post') one. This helped the West German Green party to make a breakthrough in 1983 when it scored 5.6 per cent of the vote and put twenty-eight MPs into the Bundestag. The votes translate into that number of seats because the Greens breached the threshold of 5 per cent and seats were then allocated proportionally to votes won. In the first past the post UK system it would be possible to win 5.6 per cent of the vote and gain no seats because the votes could be spread around the country, meaning they were not sufficiently concentrated in any one constituency to gain a majority there. In part because of the UK's unfriendly political opportunity structure, it took the

English, Welsh, and Northern Irish Greens (Scotland has its own Green party) until 2010 to have their first MP elected, Caroline Lucas.

We can see how much difference a proportional system makes by looking at the New Zealand experience. New Zealand operated a majoritarian system until 1996 when a mixed-member proportional system was voted in by referendum. Until then the Greens had won no seats in Parliament, but in 1996 they won three seats as part of the left-wing Alliance grouping, and then seven seats on their own in 1999—each time with a smaller number of votes than in the pre-proportional days. Since then the Green vote has oscillated, but it reached double figures in 2011 and 2014 (11.1 per cent and 10.7 per cent, respectively), lending some credence to the idea of a 'ratchet' effect—i.e., that once voters see that every vote for the Greens counts (which it doesn't in a majoritarian system), more people will be inclined to vote for them.

Environmental policy-making—the challenges

Whether it is Greens or mainstream parties in government or in coalition, policy-makers are confronted with a series of big challenges when it comes to making effective environmental policy. What are these challenges? And what are the policy tools that politicians have at their disposal to meet them? As far as challenges are concerned, environmental problems have characteristics that can make them especially difficult. First, they can be very complex. This is not so much a feature of the problems themselves, but of their interrelatedness. When discussing the 'limits to growth' report in Chapter 2, we noted how trying to solve environmental problems discretely could lead to not solving them at all—and even to creating new problems. The structure of government tends to militate against the co-ordinated policy-making that environmental problems demand—the government apparatus is organized around departments, each with separate responsibilities such as foreign affairs, finance, defence, and environment.

The complexity of environmental problems brings with it another troubling characteristic: uncertainty. One of the main concerns about genetic modification for some, for example, is that its effects on the 'natural' environment cannot be predicted with sufficient accuracy to make it a safe technology. Environmental policy issues are thus threaded through with the notion of risk and how best to manage it. Sometimes these types of risk are called 'manufactured' risks to distinguish them from natural risks like earthquakes, and for some they are a key defining feature of modern societies.

Another further notable characteristic of some environmental problems is their irreversibility, or at least the very long time it could take to restore a previous equilibrium. Species extinction is an example of irreversibility, and there is a host of examples of near-irreversible situations, including climate change (even if CO_2 emissions were halted tomorrow, elevated levels of carbon dioxide would remain in the atmosphere for many hundreds, even thousands, of years); and clearcutting a climax forest (this cuts off a process that has taken centuries to develop).

Drawing on a discussion we had in Chapter 1, we can see that irreversibility is linked to substitutability. For example, honey bee populations have been dying off at an increasing rate in Europe and North America in recent years—some colonies by up to 70 per cent. Many of the crops we depend on require pollination, and bees are one of nature's best pollinators—it is said that bees are responsible for one out of every three bites of food we eat. If bees were to go extinct, the change would be to all intents and purposes irreversible—but would it matter? From the point of view of function, maybe it wouldn't, since the function of pollination can be carried out in many ways—including by human hand. This is to say that the bees are substitutable, as far as their pollinating function is concerned. But if bees have value beyond the function they perform—value in themselves—then their irreversible loss will be keenly felt.

Problems with this combination of complexity, uncertainty, and irreversibility are sometimes described as 'wicked' problems (as distinct from the 'tame' ones in chess or mathematics, which, while they may be very difficult, admit of a determinate solution that can be agreed on by everyone). How should such problems be dealt with? One approach is to put precaution at the heart of the process. This has led to the development of the precautionary principle (originally *Vorsorgeprinzip* in German), a central feature of environmental policy-making, which states that the burden of proof that a course of action is not harmful lies with those taking the action. This reverses the usual dynamic, which lodges the burden of proof with the potential victims of an action. The precautionary principle also encourages policy-makers to look for alternatives to whatever course of action is causing concern. Typical areas where the precautionary principle can be deployed are global warming, food safety, genetic modification, and species extinction.

One further challenge for policy-makers is that many environmental problems involve what are called 'common-pool resources'. Common-pool resources are those no-one can be excluded from using because it would be impractical to do so. No-one can be excluded from breathing the air, for example, and while the sea can in some sense be 'owned'—coastal states have a 200-nautical-mile Exclusive Economic Zone around them—to all intents and purposes the oceans are non-divisible. Common-pool resources are a problem for policy-makers because they are hard to look after, and this is because they are subject to the 'free-rider problem': people can't be excluded from benefiting from the resource, and therefore have no self-interested reason for keeping it well-maintained. In fact, their self-interest lies in relying on other people to maintain it while they use it. The common-pool resource problem was vividly illustrated in Garrett Hardin's famous 1968 essay, 'The Tragedy of the Commons'. Hardin argued that people pursuing their self-interest in an unregulated, open-access commons of finite size would end in resource exhaustion. Hardin's solution was 'mutual coercion, mutually agreed upon by the majority of people affected'. This potentially democratic but probably illiberal solution to the free-rider problem is not the only one, and we will look at others shortly.

Environmental policy tools

Environmental policy aims to change people's individual and collective behaviour in relation to the environment, both as 'nature' and as 'resources'. What tools do politicians have at their disposal to do this? The essential context for an answer to this question is the distinction between *government* and *governance*. Government is what most people think politics is about—elected politicians passing legislation, creating regulations, and mounting information campaigns in the expectation that citizens will comply with the legislation and regulations and react appropriately to the information they have been given. This is sometimes characterized as a top-down approach to policy-making. Governance, on the other hand, refers to networks of organizations, interdependent to a greater or lesser degree, and relatively autonomous of government. It is also linked to an increasing role for the market, as opposed to the state, as the context and arena for decision-making. From a governance point of view, individuals are seen as enacting policy rather than acting out policy, as in the government model. This enacting is seen in terms of choosing the right behaviour option from a range of possibilities, with the individual 'steered' in the right direction by signals such as price. As neoliberalism has come to hold sway in the global North, and the state and 'big government' as agents of change have come to be regarded with suspicion, governance has overtaken government as the modus operandi of choice, and this has had a significant effect on all areas of policy, including the environment.

An example of government as opposed to governance would be legislating on exhaust emissions standards for road vehicles. Vehicle users have no choice but to comply with these standards. Similarly, a classic government-led information drive was the Act on CO_2 campaign launched by the UK government in 2007. This was a multimedia communication and marketing campaign to raise awareness of the contribution individuals make to CO_2 emissions, and the ways in which they can act to help tackle climate change. The campaign carried simple messages to encourage individuals to take action on carbon dioxide emissions (often saving them money too) by, for example, walking a short distance rather than driving; drying clothes outside rather than in a machine; and only part-filling a kettle. No analysis of the effectiveness of this campaign was carried out, but one of the obvious flaws with top-down information is that people will not always act on it. It also adopts what has been called the 'information deficit' model of changing behaviour, working on the assumption that the main obstacle to pro-environmental behaviour is people not knowing enough, or not knowing the right things. This forgets that such behaviour requires a supportive and effective infrastructure—the citizen may well understand that it is good to recycle glass bottles, but is unable to do so because the facilities for doing so aren't available.

Another policy tool for government is, of course, taxation. One can tax users, emissions, or products to encourage more pro-environmental practices. So rubbish can be taxed to discourage people from throwing it away, pollutants can be taxed to discourage their emission, and plastic bags can be taxed to discourage their use. One observed disadvantage of the taxation approach is that, so long as taxes are regarded as a bad thing, it inexorably links the environment with punishment, and while this might work in the short term it fails to generate the buy-in for long-term, good sustainability practice. Also, environmental taxes of this sort tend to be regressive—that is, they hit the poor hardest. So in the absence of a broader set of redistributive fiscal policies—a progressive income tax, for example—taxation for sustainability can tend towards injustice.

In general, 'government' (as opposed to governance) leads to a focus on implementation, and the intractability of many environmental problems means that governments often fall short of expectations. One way for governments to avoid this environmental 'implementation gap' is to 'download' responsibility to interdependent organizations outside government, and to individuals—in other words, to exchange government for governance. So instead of legislating for fixed exhaust emission standards, a governance approach would allow vehicle users a range of options to choose from. In the UK, for example, the compulsory road tax payment is banded according to CO_2 emissions, thus giving car owners a choice of vehicle—as long as they are prepared to (and can) pay the CO_2 premium. This approach is more consistent with the so-called choice agenda of modern liberal capitalist societies than one-size-fits-all legislation, but whether it is more effective is an open question.

Pricing nature

One increasingly popular approach, consistent with governance rather than government, to meeting the challenge of nature conservation is to put a price on nature. This often goes hand-in-hand with thinking of nature as providing a set of services—'ecosystem services'. Rather than treating these services as a free good, and therefore effectively encouraging their overuse and discouraging their care and protection, putting a price on them ensures (in theory) that they will be taken account of in analyses of costs and benefits. In economics terms this is sometimes called 'internalizing the externalities'. A negative externality occurs when a cost is imposed by a producer or a consumer on a third party, for which the producer or consumer cannot be charged. An example might be a riparian (riverside) farmer using chemical pesticides which then flow into the river adjoining his or her land. The residues are then washed downstream where they can cause health problems for humans and other animals. Left to its own devices, the market doesn't include the negative external costs of the farmer's activities upstream imposed on those living downstream. Put differently, the costs and benefits of this agricultural sub-system will not be fully accounted for until a price is put on this negative externality. This could be done by taxing the chemical pesticides to discourage the farmer from using them, or by putting a price (value) on the water used by the people living downstream.

Picking up an earlier example, the economic value of honey bees and bumble bees as pollinators has been estimated at £200 million ($304 million or €269 million) per year to the UK economy. Honey bee populations are in decline because of certain farming practices and because of the varroa mite. Improving these practices and dealing with the mite would cost money, but the point of putting a price on the 'ecosystem service' the bees perform is to enable a more complete and rounded calculation of the costs and benefits of doing so. This might make the £200 million seem money well spent.

One difficulty with this approach to looking after nature—putting a price on it—is working out how much it is worth. Normally, the price of something is determined by what people are prepared to pay for it in the market place. This presupposes that the thing is being traded, but one of the reasons why 'ecosystem services' are so often free is, precisely, because they are not traded. So how do we arrive at a price for them? A common technique is to use 'shadow pricing', which involves asking people what they would be prepared to pay for a non-traded service (this is sometimes called 'willingness to pay'), or what they would be prepared to accept in compensation for consuming an undesirable good. An environmental example of the former might be the preservation of a local park, while the latter could relate to compensation paid to residents near a fracking site. The shadow price contains three elements—the use value, option value, and existence value of an amenity. Use value is what we would pay for an amenity—using the park for walking the dog or playing Frisbee, for example. Option value is the value we put on some future use of the amenity—building an aviary in the park, for example, would potentially increase its value. Existence value is the value we put on something even if it has no obvious use or option value. The total value of the amenity or service is obtained by adding all these together. If a municipal council is approached by a developer with a view to building an apartment block on or near the park, the cost–benefit analysis must take into account this 'shadow value'.

Is this an 'accurate' value? One objection to the shadow pricing exercise is that it might be skewed by a biased sample. Bird enthusiasts will put a higher option value on the park if it's to contain an aviary than those who would rather see a skateboard park. If the sample of respondents contains plenty of ornithologists and few skateboarders, the option value will be greater than it 'should' be. A second objection is that people tend to put a higher value on an amenity or a service when they know they are not actually going to have to pay for it. A third objection is that it is wrong in principle to put a price on nature; thinking of nature as something that can be bought, sold, and traded is part of the problem rather than part of the solution, as this reduces the diversity and variety of nature to one 'substance'—money.

More generally, critics say that there is a problem with trying to achieve sustainability by trading different bits of nature off against each other. There is increasing support in policy-making circles for what is called 'biodiversity offsetting'. The basic idea is that if development in one place is likely to reduce biodiversity, then that damage can be compensated for by protecting or enhancing biodiversity elsewhere. As the UK government puts it: 'when a development damages nature (and this damage cannot be avoided) new, bigger, or better nature sites will be created'. This inevitably raises the question of how we judge 'better'. Is a honey bee better than a swift or a swallow? UK government guidelines say that if a habitat of 'low' distinctiveness (itself an awkward judgement to make) is to be disturbed by development, then any offsetting should 'trade up'. This apparently laudable objective is undermined for some by: (a) the difficulty in deciding what 'trading up' might actually mean in terms of species and habitats; and (b) the very use of the language of commerce to describe the process, implying that the diversity of nature can be reduced to a single metric.

Cap-and-trade

Shadow pricing involves an imaginary market place. Another possibility is to create a real market in some environmental 'good' or 'bad', and trade it. Take, for example, the challenge of reducing carbon emissions. One approach is to put a cap on the total emissions allowable, and then allocate or sell permits to carbon-emitting industries up to the total. If a firm needs to emit more than its permits allow, it can buy extra permits from firms that are under-emitting. If this works well the cap is respected, and there is an incentive for firms to reduce their emissions so that they can sell permits to other firms. While 'cap-and-trade' (as it is known) generally applies to firms, the principle can also be applied to individual citizens in the form of what is often called a 'carbon card'. Each citizen is given a quota of carbon emissions for a year, say, and each time he or she purchases a good or a service with carbon 'embedded' in it, some of the quota is used up. As with firm-level cap-and-trade, those who underuse their quota can sell the surplus to those who are overemitting carbon—or who wish to do so. Given that there is a correlation between wealth/income and carbon emissions, the carbon card could result in a significant redistribution of wealth as those with carbon-intensive lifestyles purchase the 'privilege' of leading such a lifestyle from those who consume less carbon.

While cap-and-trade sounds like an ideal combination of government (the imposition of caps/quotas) and governance (a degree of flexibility and choice as to how to meet the cap/quote requirements), there are four difficulties with it. First, there will be disagreements over the cap—the science points towards quite stringent caps, while the interest of carbon-emitting firms obviously lies in keeping the cap as loose and as high as possible. Second, the original distribution of permits is critical—they must be neither so numerous nor so cheap that they lose their potential for creating carbon discipline. One criticism of the European Emissions Trading System (ETS) is that it bequeathed windfall rights to the biggest carbon polluters rather than dividing them up more equally among relevant stakeholders—including citizens. Third, some cap-and-trade arrangements allow participants to 'offset' their carbon emissions by investing in carbon reduction schemes outside the cap-and-trade zone. Offset schemes are themselves very controversial, and are often regarded as a way of outsourcing carbon emissions rather than reducing them. Finally, cap-and-trade is subject to the 'too far downstream' critique. Upstream, the fossil fuel is removed from the ground; and downstream, it is consumed. Upstream it is easy to control—one simply closes the mine or shuts off the borehole. The further one moves downstream, the harder the use of carbon is to control because of the constant multiplication of users. Like most governance approaches, cap-and-trade is a downstream policy tool, which, while suiting the flexibility and choice agendas of modern government, is subject to complexities around implementation.

Financial incentives and environmental citizenship

The furthest downstream one can go is the individual liver-of-a-life—each and every one of us. We all have an 'environmental footprint'—an impact on the world around us. Governments are increasingly keen to influence the nature and size of that footprint by creating a framework of incentives and disincentives which are designed to encourage us towards environmentally friendly behaviours and practices. The common currency of this framework is money, in the form of a series of fines and rewards designed to steer people towards more pro-environmental behaviour. Faced with the challenge of reducing congestion in city centres in Singapore, London, and Milan, for example, planners have introduced congestion charges which require drivers to pay a fee to drive in the city centre at certain times and on certain days. As we observed with environmental taxation at the level of the individual, these charges can be regressive, and the policy tool has also been criticized for discouraging a deeper engagement with environmental problems by asking users to respond to price signals rather than the sustainability issue they are designed to deal with. What would happen if the congestion charge was suspended? Most of us answer that people would revert to driving into the city centre rather than take the alternatives. This illustrates both the strengths and weaknesses of the fine/reward approach: the strength is that it works quickly, while the weakness is that it may work only for as long as the regime of fines and rewards is in place.

Financial incentives/disincentives are a one-size-fits-all policy tool—everyone is regarded as being susceptible to financial inducements and penalties. Beyond this, policy-makers recognize that people have a varying willingness to act pro-environmentally, and different capacities for doing so. This leads to a 'social marketing' approach to environment-related behaviour change. In much the same way as supermarkets gather information on their customers in order to tailor their offer more effectively, the UK government—for one—has adopted a social marketing approach, dividing the population into seven segments according to their willingness to act pro-environmentally and their recipients' aspirations and capacities. So while a 'positive Green' (one of the segments) might be prepared to pioneer a new technology—install solar panels, for example—the 'stalled starter' (another segment) would need the technology to be much more normalized and widespread before taking action.

A common thread in all the policy tools discussed thus far is that they assume that people will act only reluctantly in favour of the environment. There is evidence, though, from practices such as ethical investment that some citizens are prepared to take a financial hit for pro-sustainability reasons. These people invest their money in funds that are screened to avoid supporting environmentally damaging activities, such as the fossil fuel industry or nuclear power, and are prepared to make significant losses for ethical reasons. This has led to the development of the idea of 'environmental citizenship', which, while generally absent from the governmental' policy toolbox, captures something of the motivations of the small but important segment of the population that 'pioneers' new practices for sustainability.

What this chapter shows is that in a relatively short space of time—about fifty years—environmental problems have given rise to an impressive array of political actors dedicated to dealing with them, and the development by national governments of policy tools for sustainability. But environmental problems have an international—even a global—character. Environmental politics is therefore, at least in part, an international politics, and so Chapter 4 is about how the national and international dimensions work—or not—together.

Chapter 4
Local and global, North and South

By 1648, territories in the Holy Roman Empire had been at war for thirty years, and the Spanish and Dutch for eighty years. In that year the Westphalian Treaty was signed. This treaty established a principle that has influenced national and international politics ever since—the principle of sovereignty. In 1648 this involved the right of rulers to determine the religion of their subjects, and by 1918 it had come to embody the broader idea that nation states have a right to determine their own affairs without interference from other states. The principle spread from its European origins and was eventually a driving force behind the decolonization process that freed countries from colonial rule during the second half of the 20th century.

The principle is a powerful and important one for obvious reasons, and it has a special relevance in the context of environmental politics. Environmental problems are famously borderless, and this complicates the principle of national self-determination that is at the heart of international politics. For an increasing number of people in the world (though still a minority) our very lives are increasingly borderless. The components in your laptop come from up to sixteen different countries, your trainers might be made in Vietnam, your tea from Kenya. So complex is the sourcing of materials, the process of putting them together, and shipping and marketing them, that it took Pietra Rivoli years to research *The Travels of a T-Shirt in the Global Economy*. Another way of illustrating the borderless character of much modern production and consumption is through the idea of the 'ecological footprint'. Each of us has an impact on the Earth in terms of the resources we use and the waste we produce—this is our ecological footprint. The ecological space our footprint occupies is obviously not confined to our immediate surroundings—we 'borrow' space from elsewhere. A glance at the contents of your refrigerator or wardrobe will confirm this. The more globalized our lives are, the more 'smeared' our footprint is across the planet.

Globalization

In this sense, environmental politics is an international politics—even a global politics. In his book *The End of Nature* (1989), Bill McKibben argues that what marks out the contemporary world from any previous period of human history is, precisely, the capacity humans have for influencing their environment at a *global* level. Global warming, he says, is exactly that—global. We have now altered 'every inch and every hour of the globe':

> If you travel by plane and dog team and snowshoe to the farthest corner of the Arctic and it is a mild summer day, you will not know whether the temperature is what it is 'supposed' to be, or whether, thanks to the extra carbon dioxide, you are standing in the equivalent of a heated room.

This is the environmental version of what has come to be called 'globalization'—the phenomenon which is so especially in tension with the principle of national sovereignty enshrined in the Westphalian Treaty of 1648. It has also led to the suggestion that human impact on the environment is so far-reaching that we have

6. A child recycling e-waste in Guiyu, China: one aspect of globalization.

set in train a new geological epoch—the Anthropocene. We will look at this further in Chapter 5.

In a classic definition, David Held talks of globalization as the 'widening, intensifying, speeding up and growing impact of world-wide interconnectedness'. Obviously this process is not uniform, in terms of either speed or impact; it is not symmetrical. Indian feminist and environmentalist Vandana Shiva argues that the asymmetry of globalization takes a particular form—one in which the global North globalizes while the global South *is globalized* (see Figure 6):

> The construction of the global environment narrows the South's options while increasing the North's. Through its global reach, the North exists in the South, but the South exists only within itself, since it has no global reach. Thus the South can *only* exist locally, while only the North exists globally.

Global warming is a good example of this asymmetry at work, as can be seen in Table 2.

Table 2. The asymmetry of the global environment

Country	CO_2 emissions per capita (in 2010)
United States	17.5
United Kingdom	8.0
Australia	16.8
Canada	14.7
Saudi Arabia	16.9
Spain	5.9
China	6.2
India	1.6
Brazil	2.2
Bangladesh	0.4
Ethiopia	0.01

Source: Millennium Development Goals indicators (2013)

In Shiva's terms these figures show that the 'North exists in the South' by imposing global warming on the South (represented by India, Brazil, Bangladesh, and Ethiopia in the table) through higher per capita emissions. This is asymmetrical globalization at work, though it is important to recognize how geo-environmental realties can shift over time—China is now a bigger aggregate CO_2 polluter than the USA, even though its per capita emissions are lower.

The role of globalization in the environmental crisis is disputed. It would be wrong to say that it has caused environmental problems as they evidently existed before the processes described by Held and Shiva got under way. But it is fair to say that increased rates of investment, trade, and production have accelerated and intensified environmental impacts around the world. Critics of this process argue that it is not just that trade volumes have increased, but that the terms of trade are such that environmental sustainability is not sufficiently taken into account. The World Trade Organization (WTO) is a key player in this regard. The WTO was founded in 1995 as a successor to the General Agreement on Tariffs and Trade (GATT) which was signed in 1947. The GATT was designed to reduce trade barriers, and the WTO's remit is similar. This creates problems around increasingly important environmental issues such as biosecurity. Biosecurity has been described as 'the attempted management or control of unruly biological matter', and it is clear how the controls and import restrictions this implies are in tension with the open market and free trade promoted by the WTO. Effective biosecurity is important from the point of view of plant, animal, and human health, and we can see from the Ebola crisis of 2014 what happens when biosecurity breaks down. The tension between free trade and biosecurity is captured in the WTO's Sanitary and Phytosanitary (SPS) agreement which states that member states have a right to impose restrictions to preserve plant, animal, or human health, but not where these measures discriminate on the grounds of process and production methods, or impose 'unnecessary, arbitrary, scientifically unjustifiable or disguised restrictions on trade'.

This is why governing plant and animal health in a neoliberal globalized world is a challenge. For example, there have been two Dutch Elm disease pandemics in the 20th century, and both were caused by the transport of infected timber. The increasingly international horticultural trade has also opened up transmission routes for plant diseases and insect pests. The WTO has a Dispute Settlement Panel where disagreements between governments trying to limit trade and companies resisting those limitations are resolved. It is significant that many of the trade disputes in recent years have been around biosecurity, including the infamous Australia/New Zealand apple dispute. Australia banned the import of New Zealand apples in 1921 on the grounds that they were a source of a bacterial infection called fire blight. In 2007

New Zealand began WTO dispute settlement procedures and the Australian ban on apple imports was overturned. It would be too simplistic to see this as a victory of free trade over environmental considerations since other factors come into play, but it is an example of the tensions between globalized trade and environmental protection.

On the other hand, globalization is also a process that has contributed to raising per capita income across the world, though very unequally and not everywhere. Some argue that this is good for the environment as it produces the wealth required to pay for better environmental protection and technologies. This theory is based on the environmental Kuznets curve, which purports to show that environmental quality decreases in the early stages of a country's development, but then improves once a certain average income is reached. This suggests that the best way for a country to improve its environmental performance is to get richer. The Kuznets curve (an inverted U-shape) is criticized on the grounds that it tends to hold for some environmental quality indicators, such as clean water and air pollution, but not for others, such as greenhouse gas emissions and the average per capita size of ecological footprints. These criticisms are important to bear in mind when considering Kuznets-based arguments for the possibility of decoupling economic growth and environmental impact (ecological modernization).

International environmental diplomacy and agreements

Whatever one thinks of globalization's role in undermining environmental protection, or, from an alternative point of view, in creating the conditions for improving it, it has been clear for some time that environmental problems have a transboundary character and therefore require—to some extent—a transboundary approach. On several occasions we have seen how important the early 1970s were to the development of contemporary environmental politics, and in the seminal year of 1972 the United Nations Conference on the Human Environment was held in Stockholm. This conference 'discussed common principles to inspire and guide the peoples of the world in the preservation and enhancement of the human environment', and it marked the beginning of extensive UN involvement in environment and sustainability issues which has lasted to this day. The next major UN-sponsored event was the World Commission on Environment and Development (1987), more commonly known as the Brundtland Commission, named after Gro Harlem Brundtland, the former Prime Minister of Norway who was chosen to chair it. The Brundtland Commission subtly changed the debate's terms of reference by talking about sustainable development rather than environmental sustainability, thereby signalling a determination to recognize that sustainability of the environment and the development of societies must go hand in hand, without privileging either of them to the detriment of the other. The Brundtland Commission gave us the most commonly used definition of sustainable development: 'Development that meets the needs of the present without compromising the ability of future generations to meet their own needs'.

The most far-reaching UN conference took place in 1992 in Rio de Janeiro, Brazil. Its official name was the United Nations Conference on Environment and Development (UNCED), but it is more popularly known as the Rio Summit. It was far-reaching because it set in train three pieces of work, the implications of which are still with us today. The first was the Convention on Biological Diversity (CBD), in which parties agreed to conserve diversity, use resources sustainably, and share the benefits of diversity fairly. The CBD picks up the Brundtland sustainable development theme, containing the idea that genetic resources should be developed—but sustainably—for the benefit of present and future generations. The second was called Agenda 21, and particularly Chapter 11 of Agenda 21, which focused on the role of local authorities in embedding sustainable development. Local

Agenda 21, as it came to be known, embodies the well-known mantra 'think global, act local', and it enjoined local actors across the world—elected officials, citizens, and businesses—to develop plans for sustainable development at the local level. Take up was inevitably patchy, and over three-quarters of the activity took place in Europe—particularly in the UK and Sweden—but where the practice took root, a legacy which legitimized local participation was created which citizens and other local actors continue to access.

The third was the most far-reaching Convention of all—the United Nations Framework Convention on Climate Change (UNFCCC). This treaty set in train the climate change negotiations which are still ongoing. Its aim was—and is—to 'stabilize greenhouse gas concentrations in the atmosphere at a level that would prevent dangerous anthropogenic interference with the climate system'. No specific limits or mechanisms were set at this point, but the signatories agreed to meet every year at a Conferences of the Parties (COP) to develop legally binding obligations. The best-known COP was the one that took place in Kyoto in 1997, and which gave rise to the Kyoto Protocol.

We will be discussing the climate change negotiations in more detail shortly in the context of an analysis of the factors that both help and hinder international environmental agreements. Any such agreement needs to overcome a series of challenges. We have already mentioned the key issue of national sovereignty: any international agreement is likely to involve some compromise as far as perceived national interest is concerned. Second, most environmental issues involve science and scientific data. While we might think that this would make for a solid bedrock on which to base agreements, the opposite tends to be the case: either the data or the conclusions drawn from them are a source of constant dispute. Third, divisions among 'developed' nations as to the best way forward are common, and this is compounded by what has until recently been an apparently insurmountable faultline between the global North and the global South. This faultline represents the tension between environmental protection on the one hand and development on the other. The global South believes that equity is a key issue in multilateral environmental negotiations, for two reasons. First, they argue that the global North has caused the lion's share of global environmental problems, and has benefited from doing so. This is why the global North should bear the brunt of the costs of protection. Second, the global South should not have to forgo development for the sake of environmental protection. Development has brought tremendous benefits to the global North, and it would be unfair to deny those benefits to the global South, especially in respect of a problem (environmental degradation) for which the global North is primarily responsible.

The fourth challenge to reaching meaningful and actionable multilateral environmental agreements (MEAs) is the multiplicity of actors in play, and in particular the capacity some have for influencing democratically elected governments. Corporations and international non-governmental organizations (INGOs) are important players in negotiations, but the power of the former far outweighs the latter, and corporations have the capacity to make or break negotiations, as we shall see shortly in the context of the Montreal Protocol on the ozone layer. The final obstacle is the growth imperative which constitutes the context for all environmental negotiations. The idea of a 'one planet economy' has very little traction at the international level; and from the point of view of the political ecologist who believes that there are limits to growth, this amounts to fighting with one hand tied behind one's back. Despite these obstacles, multilateral environmental agreements are possible, and we shall shortly be comparing and contrasting two cases—the ozone layer and climate change—to help analyse the factors and conditions that make for successful agreements. Some of the key MEAs across a range of environmental issue areas are summarized in Table 3.

What makes for a successful international environmental agreement, and what gets in the way of success? Forty years of

Table 3. Some key multilateral environmental agreements

Issue area	Name of Convention or Treaty	Date and place
Atmosphere	Convention on Long-Range Transboundary Air Pollution	Geneva, 1979
Marine living resources	Convention for the Conservation of Antarctic Marine Living Resources	Canberra, 1980
Marine environment	UN Convention on the Law of the Sea	Montego Bay, 1982
Nature conservation	Convention on Biological Diversity	Nairobi, 1992
Nuclear safety	Comprehensive Test Ban Treaty	1996
Hazardous substances	Minamata Convention on Mercury	Minamata, 2013

trial and error allow us to draw some conclusions, and attention is often drawn to two contrasting sets of negotiations with a view to outlining the factors that make success more or less likely. The negotiations in question are those around the protection of the ozone layer, on the one hand, and those around climate change, on the other. Both of these looked very difficult—even intractable—at the outset, but one resulted in a lasting and generally well-observed agreement, while the other is the subject of endless disputes that have yet to result in an agreement that satisfies both the science as well as the potential parties to the agreement. We will look at these in turn.

Ozone diplomacy—a relative success story

The ozone layer is essential for life on Earth as we know it. It is a layer in the stratosphere, between 19 and 30 kilometres above the Earth's surface, that contains high concentrations of ozone relative to the rest of the atmosphere and absorbs most of the sun's ultraviolet (UV) radiation. UV radiation causes us to tan, but an excess can increase the chances of skin cancer and eye damage. It can also harm plants and animals and, as UV rays can penetrate water, they are especially dangerous for plankton, at the base of the marine food chain. In May 1985, an article was published in *Nature* announcing an annual depletion of the ozone layer above the Antarctic—between 1955 and 1995 the ozone concentration at springtime declined by about two-thirds. In 1974 it had been suggested that ozone concentrations could be adversely affected by man-made chemicals containing chlorine, such as chlorofluorocarbons (CFCs), but also compounds containing bromine, other related halogen compounds, and nitrogen oxides (NOx). CFCs are used in refrigeration systems, air conditioners, aerosols, solvents, and some types of packaging. Nitrogen oxides are a by-product of combustion, for example from car or aircraft engines. The evidence that these chemicals were indeed causing the annual depletion in the ozone layer piled up, and in 1988 the science-based Ozone Trends Panel confirmed the connection between CFCs and ozone depletion. By this point, one key ingredient for a successful international agreement was in place: consensus on the science. Even ahead of this scientific confirmation, twenty nations signed the Vienna Convention for the Protection of the Ozone Layer in 1985, which produced no targets for limiting CFC production but did provide a framework for co-operation on the issue.

CFCs were invented in the 1920s, and by the time the danger they represented was fully understood, they had become a significant player in modern industrial economies. This meant that large chemical firms, such as ICI and Dupont, stood to lose millions of dollars from a ban on CFCs unless substitutes could be found. To begin with these firms claimed that the science behind the ozone depletion theory was faulty, but then in 1986 Dupont broke with other producers by announcing that it would back negotiations to limit CFC production. Two possible reasons have been given for this. First, the US government had banned CFCs such as Freon in aerosol cans, while a Dupont patent on Freon had in any case expired in 1979. This combination of adverse regulation and a decline in competitive advantage in the market place made continued investment in CFCs seem less attractive. Second, Dupont recognized that competitive advantage could be regained by developing substitute chemicals—this would give it first mover advantage. This led to a race with a number of other companies such as ICI to develop substitutes for CFCs which would do the same job without depleting the ozone layer. As a result, hydrofluorocarbons (HFCs) are increasingly used as substitutes. Corporations thus played a critical role in the development of an ozone agreement—without their support, neither a successful accord nor its implementation would have been as likely.

Another key element in the development of the ozone regime was the negotiating states themselves. In 1977, the so-called Toronto Group, comprising Norway, Finland, Sweden, the USA, and Canada, unilaterally banned non-essential aerosol use (asthma inhalers, for example, were exempted). European Community states, under pressure from producers responsible for up to half of world CFC production at the time, resisted any call for action until West Germany broke with the European consensus. By this point, the negotiating states, the science, and the corporations were all more or less aligned, and the Montreal Protocol on Substances that Deplete the Ozone Layer was signed in 1987. Since then, CFC concentrations have levelled out or decreased, but the sting in the tail is that their replacements, hydrofluorocarbons, contribute to global warming.

The treaty was the first universally ratified treaty in United Nations history, and this meant that an additional hurdle had to be overcome—persuading developing countries to sign up. Ozone depletion had been caused principally by the already industrialized countries, though its effects were felt by everyone. Likewise, CFCs had enabled industrialized countries to take advantage of refrigeration and other technologies in competitive markets. Why should developing countries bear the cost of solving a problem they hadn't caused? In 1990 a technology transfer fund was set up to help developing countries transition to ozone-safe production. This helped to establish the principle of 'common but differentiated responsibility'—i.e., that all states have a responsibility for dealing with global environmental problems, but that some states have more of a responsibility than others. Finally, signatories to the Protocol agreed to build sanctions into the treaty, designed to punish countries which might be tempted to leave it or break it.

This brief analysis of the Montreal Protocol helps us to identify the key features of a successful multilateral environmental agreement: a consensus on the science; a key state or states (in this case West Germany) tipping the balance in favour of agreement by disengaging from the laggards and joining the leaders; a ready alternative to the phenomenon, situation, or entity that is causing the problem; a resolution of any equity issues that might be raised by pursuing this alternative; and sanctions for transgressors.

Climate change diplomacy—a relative failure

We can helpfully contrast the relatively successful ozone story with the much more intractable issue of global warming, or climate change. Why has this proved so much more difficult a nut to crack? There are similar factors in play: scientific evidence, national sovereignty, divisions between countries in the global North, divisions between the global North and the global South, and the power of large corporations. But while it was possible to overcome the problems arising from these factors in the ozone case, it has proved much more difficult to do so with climate change. Before discussing why, we need to see what global warming is, the state of the science surrounding it, and the implications of global warming for human and other life.

Global warming—or climate change—is a result of the 'greenhouse effect'. (In what follows I will be using the terms 'climate change' and 'global warming' indistinguishably. Some have suggested that 'climate change' is too neutral a term in that it implies the possibility of temperatures going up and down—as they have done throughout the planet's history—and therefore plays into the hands of those who would say that any current change in average global temperatures is part of natural variation. The term 'global warming' makes it clear that temperatures are rising, and, given that the temperature rise coincides with the increased burning of fossil fuels since the Industrial Revolution, the conclusion that human activity is the cause of the rise.) Up to a point the greenhouse effect makes life on Earth possible—certain gases such as carbon dioxide, water vapour, methane, and nitrous oxide absorb some of the sun's radiation as it is reflected back off the Earth's surface, trapping heat in the atmosphere. Without this effect, the Earth's average surface temperature would be over 30°C lower than it is at present: roughly −18°C rather than 15°C. This wouldn't make life impossible, but it would make it very difficult. The problem is that the scientific evidence amassed over several decades strongly suggests that the balance is being upset by human activity, which is increasing the concentrations of greenhouse gases in the atmosphere, leading to a rise in average temperature at the Earth's surface. This is *anthropogenic* climate change—i.e., climate change which is caused by human beings—as distinct from any 'natural' greenhouse effect.

The body that co-ordinates the scientific evidence regarding climate change is called the Intergovernmental Panel on Climate Change (IPCC), founded in 1988 under the auspices of the United Nations. The IPCC has published five assessment reports (1990, 1992, 1995, 2001, and 2014) reviewing the latest climate science. IPCC reports are broadly accepted by governments around the world and the evidence they gather provides the basis for the climate change negotiations we will be discussing shortly. There is resistance to the idea of anthropogenic climate change, though, in the form of 'climate scepticism'. Climate sceptics lodge three doubts: first, they query the reasons for the increase in temperature, and in particular the way in which temperature rise is supposed to follow increases in greenhouse gases concentrations; second, whether the temperature rise exceeds normal variation; and third, whether human activity is the principal cause of the observed warming. A related objection is that even if anthropogenic climate change exists, overall human welfare would be more greatly increased if, instead of spending money on mitigating climate change, we spent it on finding a vaccination for malaria or providing clean water for the billions of people who don't have it. This argument is most powerfully and controversially put in Bjørn Lomborg's *The Skeptical Environmentalist*.

In response to the climate sceptics, 97 per cent of scientists say that it is very likely that human activity is causing global warming, and the main conclusions of the IPCC's latest Summary for Policymakers are collected in Box 1. But while the science of climate change might be settled, the politics of the science certainly is not. Climate scepticism tends to follow political cleavages, with scepticism more common on the right than the left. It is particularly prevalent in the USA, where Republicans have been active in promoting scepticism, though there are also loud sceptical voices in the UK and Australia.

Box 1 IPCC—selected conclusions from the 'Summary for Policymakers'

- Warming of the climate system is unequivocal, and since the 1950s, many of the observed changes are unprecedented over decades to millennia. The atmosphere and ocean have warmed, the amounts of snow and ice have diminished, the sea level has risen, and the concentrations of greenhouse gases have increased.
- Each of the last three decades has been successively warmer at the Earth's surface than any preceding decade since 1850.

Box 1 Continued

- Ocean warming dominates the increase in energy stored in the climate system, accounting for more than 90 per cent of the energy accumulated between 1971 and 2010.
- Over the last two decades, the Greenland and Antarctic ice sheets have been losing mass, glaciers have continued to shrink almost worldwide, and Arctic sea ice and northern hemisphere spring snow cover have continued to decrease in extent.
- The rate of sea level rise since the mid-19th century has been larger than the mean rate during the previous two millennia.
- The atmospheric concentrations of carbon dioxide, methane, and nitrous oxide have increased to levels unprecedented in at least the last 800,000 years. Carbon dioxide concentrations have increased by 40 per cent since pre-industrial times, primarily from fossil fuel emissions and secondarily from net land use change emissions. The ocean has absorbed about 30 per cent of the emitted anthropogenic carbon dioxide, causing ocean acidification.
- Human influence on the climate system is clear. It is extremely likely that human influence has been the dominant cause of the observed warming since the mid-20th century.
- Most aspects of climate change will persist for many centuries even if emissions of CO_2 are stopped.
- Continued emissions of greenhouse gases will cause further warming and changes in all components of the climate system. Limiting climate change will require substantial and sustained reductions of greenhouse gas emissions.

Even though the phenomenon of anthropogenic climate change is now accepted by the vast majority of scientists, there is still uncertainty around two key questions: by how much will the Earth's average surface temperature rise; and what will the consequences of this rise be? Given the uncertainties around these questions, the IPCC and others have developed scenarios to illustrate the

Table 4. Possible global warming scenarios

CO_2 equivalent ppm range			Global average temperature warming (°C)
Lowest possible	Best estimate	Highest possible	
320	340	380	1
370	430	540	2
440	540	760	3
530	670	1,060	4
620	840	1,490	5

Source: *Warming world: impacts by degree* (Based on the National Research Council report, *Climate Stabilization Targets: Emissions, Concentrations, and Impacts over Decades to Millennia*, 2011), p. 14

possibilities. The answer to the first question is closely linked to the concentrations of CO_2 equivalent gases in the atmosphere ('CO_2 equivalent' is a way of making the calculations easier by translating the effect of each of the greenhouse gases into CO_2 terms). The Program for Climate Model Diagnosis and Intercomparison, working out of the Lawrence Livermore National Laboratory in San Francisco, has devised the scenarios laid out in Table 4.

We can put the CO_2 equivalent figures into perspective by seeing that the pre-industrial parts per million (ppm) level was 280ppm, and the highest it has ever been in the last 800,000 years is 300ppm. In March 2015, the concentration was at 401.52ppm (based on data from the Mauna Loa observatory, Hawaii), so we are already in the range at which we can expect 2°C of warming.

The other key figure in the table is the one in the right-hand column—the average temperature rise we can expect given certain CO_2 equivalent concentrations. But what do these potential rises mean in terms of their effect on human and other life? Predictions are hard to make, in part because rises in temperature will not be

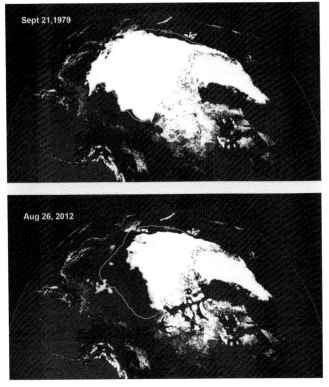

Sept 21,1979

Aug 26, 2012

7. **Decline in summer ice in the Arctic between 1979 and 2012.**

uniform across the world: land warms quicker than the oceans, and high latitudes (particularly the Arctic) will experience greater temperature increases (see Figure 7). Bearing this in mind, in 2007 (updated 2013) the UK's Meteorological Office assessed the likely impact of a 4°C rise across a range of issue areas such as sea level rise, health, agriculture, water availability, and the marine environment. Among other effects, the Met Office predicts a 60 per cent chance of irreversible decline of the Greenland ice sheet, bringing about a 7-metre sea level rise; hottest days of the year could be as much as 8°C hotter in Europe and 10–12°C hotter in

Eastern North America; ocean acidification will affect fisheries and coral reefs and those whose livelihoods depend on them; rice yields will decrease by up to 30 per cent in China, India, Bangladesh, and Indonesia; and there will be an increase in diarrhoea, dengue fever, malaria, and malnutrition, as well as the health-related impacts of weather effects such as flooding and drought.

All this gives us a picture of the latest climate science evidence and its implications. This evidence suggests that we are on the way to dangerous levels of global warming, and that greenhouse gas emissions need to be reduced. From an environmental politics point of view, the challenge is how to reduce these emissions given an international political system comprising sovereign nation states, some disagreement over the science, divisions among 'developed' countries, divisions between North and South, and the interests of the fossil fuel lobby in keeping the present system going.

Climate change first made its entry into the international arena in treaty terms at the Rio Summit in 1992, with the United Nations Framework Convention on Climate Change (UNFCCC). By this time, a degree of scientific consensus had been achieved through the first IPCC report in 1990—what was missing was a policy response from governments. The UNFCCC contained no binding agreements, except on reporting, but governments did commit to a succession of Conferences of the Parties (COPs) at which they would set targets and make commitments. The best known of these is COP-3—the Kyoto Protocol of 1997—where a legally binding commitment by developed countries to reduce greenhouse gas emissions by an average of 5 per cent of 1990 levels by 2012 was agreed. Kyoto set important precedents by distinguishing between Annex 1 (developed) and non-Annex 1 (developing) countries, placing the onus to act on Annex 1 countries, and by developing the principle of common yet differentiated responsibility. It also established three market-based mechanisms for reducing emissions: a trading regime allowing Annex 1 countries to buy and sell emission credits among themselves; a Joint Implementation method by which Annex 1 countries could implement carbon savings in other Annex 1 countries in exchange for emission credits; and a Clean Development Mechanism whereby Annex 1 countries get emission credits by funding carbon-saving projects in developing countries. These 'flexible mechanisms' seem sensible in that the point is to make reductions overall rather than make them in any particular place. But they have been criticized: (a) for allowing countries off the hook by displacing responsibility; (b) because it is hard to measure the reductions achieved by these mechanisms; and (c) because their success depends on an effectively enforced global cap, which has proved difficult to establish and achieve. They also do not take into account the 'export' of emissions—up to one-third in the case of the UK—caused by the consumption of goods and services produced elsewhere.

In terms of dealing with climate change, Kyoto had—and has—its flaws. Climate science tells us that the agreed reductions are not sufficient to keep us below 2°C, the flexible mechanisms just described are not as effective as regulation and sanctions would be, and the Annex 1/non-Annex 1 split has been a source of constant aggravation. Countries of the global North, and especially the USA, regarded it as unfair to exempt industrializing countries from emission reductions, and in 2001 the USA renounced the Kyoto Protocol on the grounds that—as President George Bush (senior) put it—it was a threat to the American way of life. As the Protocol required ratification by fifty-five countries which accounted for 55 percent of the emissions of Annex 1 countries before coming into force, America's backtracking resulted in frenetic manoeuvring as governments—particularly Russia—sought to extract concessions in exchange for their signatures. The Protocol finally came into force in February 2005, a compromise agreement that had negotiated the rocky shoals of scientific uncertainty, national self-interest, and demands for global equity.

Subsequent climate negotiations have found it difficult to overcome the tensions that have been evident since the UNFCCC in 1992. COP-15 in Copenhagen (2009) was billed as a replacement for Kyoto, but it foundered on disagreement over whether industrializing countries should take independent emission reduction measures. Lumumba Di-Aping, chief negotiator for the G77 group of 130 developing countries, said the deal represented 'the lowest level of ambition you can imagine. It's nothing short of climate change scepticism in action. It locks countries into a cycle of poverty for ever', while John Sauven, executive director of Greenpeace UK, said: 'The city of Copenhagen is a crime scene tonight, with the guilty men and women fleeing to the airport'. COP-20 in Lima (December 2014) looked as though it was heading in the same direction until the very last moment when the 'common but differentiated responsibilities' principle, which had given industrializing countries a justification for not reducing emissions, had a rider added to it: 'in light of different national circumstances'. No flesh was put on the bones, though, and at the time of writing all eyes are on Paris, where in December 2015 the COP-21 objective will be to 'achieve a legally binding and universal agreement on climate, from all the nations of the world'.

Of the five factors which led to success in the ozone/CFCs negotiations, only one—scientific consensus—is present in the global warming context, and even the science is under constant (if minority) attack from climate sceptics. There has been little agreement among 'developed' states as to objectives or mechanisms, and the key state—the USA—has been a reluctant fellow-traveller in negotiations throughout (though under President Obama there are signs of a significant softening of the USA's position). The global equity problem has not been solved, and there is still debate over how to measure emissions—per capita or per country. China has the most emissions measured by country, but it is some way behind the USA and the European Union, for example, when measured on a per capita basis. Finally, there is no ready substitute for fossil fuels, as there was for CFCs, and there is no sanctionable agreement to prevent states free-riding.

In other words, even taking account of successful multilateral negotiations such as the Montreal Protocol, there is little evidence of the development of an internationalist cosmopolitanism to replace the state-centric inclinations embodied in the Westphalian Treaty with which we began this chapter. Multilateral environmental agreements are still more a demonstration of sovereignty than an abandoning of it.

Meanwhile, global emissions continue to increase—by 2.3 percent on 2013 levels, according to the Global Carbon Project (GCP). That is 61 percent higher than in the Kyoto reference year of 1990. The GCP reports that,

> Current trajectories of fossil fuel emissions are tracking some of the most carbon intensive emission scenarios used in the Intergovernmental Panel on Climate Change (IPCC). The current trajectory is tracking baseline scenarios in the latest family of IPCC scenarios that takes the planet's average temperature to about 3.2°C to 5.4°C above pre-industrial times by 2100.

The same report suggests that we are on course to use up our quota of carbon emissions, consistent with keeping temperature rise to 2°C or less, within thirty years, and that we should be aiming to keep about half of our fossil fuel reserves in the ground, consistent with the same objective. Against this background, the challenge faced by policy-makers in Paris in 2015, and beyond, is enormous.

From the global to the local

While international environmental problems like ozone depletion and global warming seem obviously to require international-level policy, this is not the only scale at which they can be confronted. Indeed, frustration at the slow progress of climate change talks at the national and international level has led to alternative approaches at sub-national level—particularly cities. Over half the world's population lives in cities—and that figure is set to grow—so it makes sense to focus on this scale of policy development and implementation. In 2005, the then Mayor of London, Ken Livingstone, invited representatives from eighteen 'megacities' (i.e., cities with a population in excess of ten million inhabitants) to a meeting to discuss measures for reducing greenhouse gases. By 2006, the network had grown to forty cities and the term 'C40Cities' was coined as a name for the group—there are now seventy affiliated cities. C40Cities climate change mitigation action is driven by the mayors of the cities, who undertake to identify measures in policy areas where they have political competence, such as water, energy, finance and development, measurement and planning, solid waste management, and transport. At this scale, action can be taken irrespective of the success or failure of talks at the international level.

Another initiative, rooted more in the formal machinery of the United Nations, is the Cities for Climate Protection (CCP) programme, founded in 1990 by the International Union of Local Authorities and the United Nations Environment Programme. The CCP programme comprises over 650 municipalities from around thirty countries, and action is taken—as in the C40Cities example—where local government has relevant competencies such as land-use planning, traffic, and housing. Both C40Cities and CCP are examples of 'non-state transnational climate action', where entities at the sub-state level work beneath and across national boundaries to achieve climate change objectives.

More broadly, we have already commented on the United Nations' recognition of the importance of the local level for the implementation of policies for sustainable development, through Local Agenda 21, developed at the Rio Summit of 1992:

> Because so many of the problems and solutions being addressed by Agenda 21 have their roots in local activities, the participation and

co-operation of local authorities will be a determining factor in fulfilling its objectives...As the level of governance closest to the people, they play a vital role in educating, mobilizing and responding to the public to promote sustainable development.

The success of Local Agenda 21 was inevitably patchy, depending as it did on the differing competences of local government across a wide variety of countries with different political systems. In some places it served to energize a relatively dormant local government (e.g., the UK), while in others it was enthusiastically taken up in countries with a tradition of strong local government (e.g., Sweden).

Underpinning these relatively formal initiatives, it is important to see that the local scale has always been important in environmental politics. The link between the local and global is captured in the well-worn phrase "think global, act local", which lends primacy of action to the local level in the belief that myriad threads of sustainable action at that level will amount to a tapestry of sustainable development at the global level. For this reason, environmental politics has always had an enduring decentralist character, and there is a creative tension between those who argue that environmental politics should be wholly local, and those who feel that the global (or at least international) character of environmental problems means that they need a response at the global level.

The localists point out, in response, that these global problems are a result of dysfunctionalities at the local level. They argue, for example, that the scalar gap between production and consumption has grown too wide to be sustainable, and that there should be more local production for local use. This gives rise to the idea of the 'prosumer' (a term coined by Alvin Toffler in *Future Shock* in 1973)—the producer who consumes what she or he produces. A good example of this in action is the allotment system in the UK, where citizens grow their own food for their own (or their friends') consumption. Allotment 'prosumers' are a growing force, and it was estimated in 2011 that there was a waiting list of nearly 100,000 would-be local food-growers in the UK. Another argument in favour of more localized politics is that it helps to generate the disposition of care for the land which is a core feature of environmental politics—'land' understood in the general sense of 'that which sustains and surrounds us'. From this point of view, care for the global environment piggybacks on care for the local environment—we are less likely to exercise the former if we don't have the opportunity to 'practise' the latter.

The local level is also crucial to environmental politics because this is where its implications are felt most viscerally and its battles are fought most keenly. Far from the air-conditioned meeting rooms of UN environment conferences and the lobbies of five-star hotels adorned with fountains and plush sofas frequented by their delegates, we find lives blighted by our failure to implement an effective politics for sustainability—or, occasionally, lives enhanced by our success in doing so. These battles are often fought over LULUs—Locally Unwanted Land Uses—and we find them all over the world. The battles are fierce because they affect people's immediate, daily lives—often their very livelihoods. This, after all, is where most people's concerns lie, most of the time. The issues with which much of this chapter has been taken up, such as biodiversity, ozone depletion, and global warming can seem far away in space and time, and are therefore crowded out by more immediate concerns. Environmental issues have a greater 'felt' relevance if they affect the family, neighbourhood, or city over the next few months or years. It is worth pointing out, though, that even the apparently remote issues of biodiversity, ozone depletion, and global warming are more immediate for some people. Examples are the indigenous inhabitants of rainforests who depend on a relatively undisturbed habitat for their livelihood, or the 400,000 Maldive islanders threatened by a climate change-induced sea level rise that could see parts of their nation underwater within a hundred years. For these people, climate change is here and now, not far away in some ill-defined future. In October 2009, President Mohamed Nasheed, then Maldives President, held a cabinet meeting underwater to draw the world's attention to his people's plight, and to urge effective action at the Copenhagen climate change summit in December that year.

LULU disputes drive some of the most contentious examples of environmental politics in action. They involve some change in local land use which is perceived as harmful to sectors of the local population. An example drawn from Europe is the siting of windfarms, to which some local people object because they spoil the view, make too much noise, or kill birds. Note that these are objections of a different type to the more generic ones regarding cost or efficiency. They are rooted in the effect the wind turbines have on the daily lives of the objectors, rather than in the more abstract reservations that anyone might have about wind turbines—even those who live nowhere near the windfarm itself. LULU disputes often come trailing another acronym—'nimby', or 'Not In My Backyard'. 'Nimby' is a pejorative term, implying as it does that the development being objected to would be acceptable if it was happening somewhere else. Local environmental disagreements can often bring people and organizations with an environmental or sustainability brief into conflict with one another. So while Friends of the Earth (UK) supports the development of onshore wind energy, the Council for the Protection of Rural England (CPRE) takes a much more cautious view: 'While wind energy can make an important contribution to tackling climate change, CPRE believes this should not come at the expense of the beauty, character and tranquillity of rural England'.

Local livelihoods, the environment, and social struggle

Local environmental disputes are often about much more than 'only' the environment, and involve issues around democracy, participation, and justice too. One example is the long-running conflict over a number of large dam projects on the Narmada River in India. Protest has focused on the largest of these, the Sardar Sarovar Dam, in Gujarat. The dam has been the subject of a series of proposals over the past thirty years to increase its height, thereby increasing the size of the reservoir, providing water for homes and industry, irrigation, and hydroelectric power. Significantly, the opposition group 'Friends of River Narmada' refers to the dam's construction as 'one of the most important *social* issues in contemporary India', rather than as an environmental issue. This is because much of the resistance to the project is rooted in a consistent lack of consultation of those affected by the plans, inadequate rehabilitation and compensation, and the way in which the plans inequitably affect the poorest and most vulnerable communities along the river. Friends of River Narmada sum up the social and environmental consequences of the development of large dams as follows: 'they have had an extremely devastating effect on the riverine ecosystem and have rendered destitute large numbers of people (whose entire sustenance and modes of living are centered around the river)'. In cases like this, defending the integrity of ecosystems is not a matter of honouring some abstract principle, but of resisting an attack on livelihoods in the here and now.

It is striking how many of these environment-related local protests in defence of livelihoods are led by women. One of the key Narmada opposition groups, for example, is Narmada Bachao Andolan (NBA), whose leading spokesperson is Medha Patkar. Patkar abandoned her PhD at the Tata Institute of Social Sciences to campaign full-time, and has carried out a number of hunger strikes in protest at land grabs, house demolitions, and dam development. She was awarded the Right Livelihood Prize in honour of her social activism in 1991. This leadership by women is striking, but perhaps, on reflection, not surprising. After all it is women who are in the forefront of carrying out, and protecting the conditions for, the reproduction of life, and are therefore most immediately aware of threats to it. Nor are these local, livelihood-orientated actions confined to the global South. In recent years a powerful 'environmental justice' movement has grown in the global North, aimed at securing a fair share of environmental resources and political recognition for the poor, the vulnerable, and the disadvantaged.

One of the most famous environmental justice actions involved another woman, Lois Gibbs, who began to notice a pattern of childhood illnesses and birth defects in the local population of Love Canal, a Niagara Falls neighbourhood (New York) in the late 1970s (see Figure 8). Gibbs led her neighbours in a battle with local, state, and federal authorities, and with business stakeholders who had much to lose if findings went against them. It turned out that the houses and schools had been built on land in which 22,000 tonnes of toxic waste had been buried by Hooker Chemicals, and after years of campaigning over 800 families were rehoused and compensated. This is just one instance of the environmental injustice which has given rise to what we saw Joan Martínez-Alier, in Chapter 2, refer to as an 'environmentalism of

8. Love Canal: a totemic campaign for environmental justice.

the poor'. Poor communities get more than their fair share of landfill sites and environmental disasters disproportionately affect the vulnerable. Hurricane Katrina, which struck the Florida coast in 2005 and devastated New Orleans, affected poor people more than wealthier ones, not because the disaster was any worse in the poorer suburbs than in the richer ones, but because the poor were less well equipped to deal with it. This is a result of a lack of political resources as well as material ones—the lack of a capacity to be heard in the political arena. From this point of view, environmental justice is as much about political recognition as it is about fair shares in environmental resources.

The title of this chapter—'Local and global, North and South'—invites us to think of the environmental politics of the 'North' as global (biodiversity, ozone depletion, global warming), and the environmental politics of the 'South' as local (the defence of livelihoods). Reflections on environmental justice strongly suggest, though, that it might be more productive to think in terms of interpenetration: the global North is present in pockets of the global South, and the global South is present in the global North. This helps us to see that the riverside dwellers of the Narmada River have far more in common with environmental justice and environmental racism activists in North America than they do with India's burgeoning middle-class. It also helps us to see that environmental politics, for all its 'newness', is intimately bound up with a 'traditional' politics of the demand for voice, recognition, and justice.

Chapter 5
Environmental futures

Fifty years ago, British Prime Minister Harold Wilson is supposed to have said that a week is a long time in politics. Right at the other end of the scale we find biologist Colin Tudge writing that, 'we cannot claim to be taking our species and our planet seriously until we acknowledge that a million years is a proper unit of political time'. Wilson's point was that politics is an unpredictable business; and Tudge's is that environmental short-termism puts politics—and indeed everything else—at risk. Environmental politics has put the long term on the map: it focuses as much on the long wavelength of human activity and its impact on the conditions for life, as on the short.

Shifting the metaphor, environmental politics asks us to use both the telescope and the microscope: the latter is vital for analysing and improving the conditions for the day-to-day maintenance of livelihoods, while the former enables us to see the comet of unsustainability that could be heading for us, capable of wiping out the possibility of there being livelihoods at all. The telescope also tells us that the possibility—though by no means the certainty—of living unsustainably began about 12,000 years ago, with the birth of agriculture, as we saw in Chapter 1. It tells us in addition that the energy source—fossil fuel—that has powered the way of life that seems to have gone on forever is in fact only around 200 years old. It also tells us that this energy source is time limited: it is a finite resource that must at some point run out. What does this mean for the civilization it has powered? Is that time limited too? Politics measured by the week can't even begin to ask this question, let alone answer it. Part of the fascination of environmental politics lies in the scale and originality of the questions it asks, as well as the wide variety of answers it offers.

The Anthropocene

The human species is just one of about nine million on the planet, but none has been able to affect its surroundings as much as we have. It is possible, indeed, that we have done enough to have a whole new geological epoch named after us—the Anthropocene. Such is our influence on the world around us that it is felt not just weekly, monthly, or even by the century but across spans of time that had hitherto been familiar only to Earth scientists. Unwittingly, unintentionally, but inexorably, our species—the human species—has turned political time into geological time. Not many readers of this book will have heard of the International Commission on Stratigraphy (ICS) but its job is an important one: to set 'global standards for the fundamental scale for expressing the history of the Earth'. The ICS has a Subcommission on Quaternary Stratigraphy (SQS), which has set up a working group to decide, by 2016, whether the Anthropocene should be considered as a geological epoch in its own right—to signal that our activities have brought to an end the current Holocene period (which has lasted 11,700 years)—or as a subdivision of the Holocene.

The term 'Anthropocene' was first coined by Paul Crutzen and Eugene Stoermer in a May 2000 article in the International Geosphere–Biosphere Programme newsletter. Taking into account the 'growing impacts of human activities on earth and atmosphere...at all, including global, scales', they wrote, 'it seems to us more than appropriate to emphasize the central role of mankind in geology and ecology by proposing to use the term "anthropocene" for the current geological epoch'. Their suggestion for an Anthropocene start date was the latter part of the 18th century, coinciding with a key driver in the origins of environmental politics we identified in Chapter 1, the Industrial Revolution. They say that human impact is not a temporary blip but is likely to last for a long time—even if we take drastic action over global warming now, its effects will last for tens of thousands of years because of momentum built into the climate system. This makes it clear that, when considering the future of environmental politics, we can confidently say that it *has* a future. Environmental politics is not some 'here today, gone tomorrow' fad, but a feature of the political landscape which, now that it is established, is likely to persist well into the future. In part this is because the problems that have given rise to it are not likely to be solved any time soon. Global warming is at present the most obvious example, but other environmental issues such as species loss, deforestation, and urban pollution are also proving long-lasting.

Problems persist

Environmental politics also has a future because of the way in which it is tied up with livelihoods, particularly in poor and vulnerable communities. Environmental politics involves broader struggles for justice, democracy, and recognition, and as long as these struggles are ongoing—and they show no sign of abating—there will be an environmental component to them. In this context it is instructive to look at progress towards the Millennium Development Goals (MDGs). The goals were: eradicating extreme poverty and hunger; achieving universal primary education; promoting gender equality and empowering women; reducing child mortality; improving maternal health; combating HIV/AIDS, malaria, and other diseases; ensuring environmental sustainability; and developing a global partnership for development. The 2014 MDG report noted that progress had been made in a number of these areas (reduction in the number of people living in poverty, though still far too many; greater number of women in parliaments across the world; more widespread primary school education)—but that there was less progress in others. Significantly, the least progress has taken place in relation to key environmental sustainability indicators (forest loss, greenhouse gas emissions). This is more evidence for a long-term future for environmental politics, in part because the problems that gave rise to it persist. But more importantly, perhaps, it is because of a growing understanding that the various MDGs relate to one another. From this point of view it is a mistake to see the environmental sustainability goal as separate from the other seven. Indeed there is explicit recognition of this in the MDGs, with 'improved sanitation' and 'clean drinking water' as indicators of environmental sustainability. Part of the future of environmental politics, then, lies in understanding the connections between 'environmental' and 'social' goals, and developing a politics that is 'more-than-environmental'.

Poverty and wealth can both play a key role in this 'more-than-environmental' politics. Both are drivers of environmental unsustainability, for different reasons, and both provide standpoints from which to understand different dimensions of unsustainability. Poor people are often forced to degrade their environments in order to scratch a living, but out of sheer necessity they are often also the best stewards of their immediate environment because of their dependence on it for their livelihoods. Wealthy people and societies are also drivers of unsustainability—most flying and long-distance train travel, for example, is done by the A and B social classes, and hyper connectedness in the form of actual physical movement across large distances in a short space of time is the privilege of a small number of people. In the long run, the solution may lie in what has been called 'contraction and convergence', where wealthy societies contract their economies in line with limits to growth, poorer societies expand theirs in line with legitimate expectations of growth, and both eventually converge on a scale of production and consumption that satisfies both environmental sustainability and social equity.

Reform

So the problems that gave rise to environmental politics persist, and that is one reason why environmental politics has a future. A second reason is that there will always be disagreement as to how to deal with these problems. If we take an issue like global warming we can see that there are two broad approaches to solving it, and each involves a different type of environmental politics—a modified 'business-as-usual' on the one hand, and quite dramatically altered forms of life on the other. The former puts its faith in human technological ingenuity. This approach ranges from the 'ecological modernization' we looked at in Chapter 2, involving doing the same things we are doing now but more efficiently, to more drastic interventions involving the development of whole new technologies. In 2012 the United States Environmental Protection Agency (EPA) estimated that 28 percent of US greenhouse gas emissions came from transportation. From an ecological modernization point of view, this figure can be reduced by making vehicle engines more efficient in carbon emission terms. Vehicle-related greenhouse gas emissions have indeed been driven down in recent years, but as the EPA notes, transport emissions have still increased by about 18 percent since 1990 due to an increased demand for travel. In this sense, ecological modernization is always playing catch-up with increased demand for goods and services.

This suggests that perhaps more dramatic technological interventions are required. Some scientists talk of 'geo-engineering' solutions to the global warming problem—for example, heat shields placed in orbit around the Earth to deflect the sun's radiation back out into space. Research suggests that deflecting just 8 percent of the sun's radiation in this way would compensate for the effects of anthropogenic global warming on the planet. Another idea is to increase the number of phytoplankton by seeding the oceans with iron filings, thus providing the nutrients on which the plankton thrive. Plankton absorb CO_2, which in theory they take with them to the ocean floor when they die. One less far-fetched technology that has been mooted for some time is carbon capture and storage (CCS). Advocates of this unproven technology say that up to 90 percent of the carbon produced in electricity generation and industrial processes can be captured and stored. The process involves capturing it at the point of production, transporting it, and then storing it in secure underground locations. So far the prohibitive cost of CSS technology, the difficulties of retro fitting already existing industrial and power plants, and—ironically—the increased energy input it requires, have prevented its large-scale use, though some governments are vigorously pursuing it as a carbon mitigation option. The UK government, for example, has committed over £1 billion ($1.52 billion or €1.34 billion) to tendering for the commercialization of CCS, and to a dedicated research, development, and innovation programme.

Radicalism

The key point about these various solutions to global warming is that they would allow life as we know it in the industrial and post-industrial global North to go on pretty much unchanged. Sceptics, though, point out that global carbon emissions seem to rise inexorably despite our best ecological modernization efforts, and that the warnings of the Intergovernmental Panel on Climate Change (IPCC) scientists are ever more dire. In its latest (2014) report the IPCC said that to give us a better than 50 percent chance of staying below an average of 2°C of warming, our cumulative carbon emissions between 2011 and 2050 would have to be limited to about 870–1,240 gigatonnes of CO_2. This is our 'carbon budget'. The problem is that our remaining fossil fuel reserves amount to about 11,000 gigatonnes of CO_2 equivalent—between nine and thirteen times more than our carbon budget allows. A recent (2015) report in the journal *Nature* argues that, to remain within our budget, a third of oil reserves, half of gas reserves, and four-fifths of coal reserves would have to remain unused between now and 2050. The report's authors say that this would 'have profound implications for the future utilization of oil, gas and coal'. This is true—and it would also have profound implications for our daily lives since almost everything we do would be affected by the reduction in fossil fuel use this would imply. At this point, environmental politics becomes less about changing the world to fit our lives, and more about changing our lives to fit the world.

Until recently the concern was that we do not have sufficient fossil fuel resources to continue on the path we have trodden since the beginning of the Industrial Revolution. These very recent reports suggest, though, that we might have too much rather than too little, because if all of it is burnt we are heading into the territory of 5°C of warming. Thus far, policy-makers have focused on 'downstream' policy tools as far as climate change is concerned, hoping to influence the behaviour of firms, organizations, and individuals once the coal, oil, or gas is out of the ground. The IPCC's latest report implies that these policy tools are not up to the task; what we need are policies to ensure that the resource stays in the ground. Bearing all this in mind, the future of environmental politics is likely to be a battleground between those who focus on managing the consumption of fossil fuels and those who wish to scale back their production.

This faultline will be matched by arguments over the implications for daily life of these alternative paths. The latter potentially entails a major change of course, away from a politics of growth and towards a politics of sufficiency (see Figure 9). The advent of 'peak oil' has given rise to the theory of 'degrowth'. Degrowth has been defined by the academic association 'Research and Degrowth' as:

> a downscaling of production and consumption that increases human well-being and enhances ecological conditions and equity

9. **Alternative futures.**

on the planet. It calls for a future where societies live within their
ecological means, with open, localized economies and resources
more equally distributed through new forms of democratic
institutions. Such societies will no longer have to 'grow or die'.
Material accumulation will no longer hold a prime position in the
population's cultural imaginary. The primacy of efficiency will be
substituted by a focus on sufficiency, and innovation will no longer
focus on technology for technology's sake but will concentrate on
new social and technical arrangements that will enable us to live
convivially and frugally. Degrowth does not only challenge the
centrality of GDP [gross domestic product] as an overarching
policy objective but proposes a framework for transformation to a
lower and sustainable level of production and consumption, a

shrinking of the economic system to leave more space for human cooperation and ecosystems.

This is evidently a big challenge to the business-as-usual of greater environmental efficiency, downstream policy tools, and individual behaviour change. The distinction between green radicals and reformists dominated much of the early years of contemporary environmental politics up until the early 1990s, and it seemed to have been settled in favour of the latter with the development of the idea of ecological modernization and the adoption of a light-green politics by mainstream political parties. Peak oil and the increasingly alarming reports from the IPCC, though, have rejuvenated radicalism.

A mass movement?

Another feature of early contemporary environmental politics was an energetic debate over the role of democracy in environmental politics. The *Limits to Growth* report implied massive changes in politics, society, and economics, and there were those who argued that people would not submit voluntarily to the sacrifices that a scaled-down economy seemed to imply. This gave rise to 'eco-authoritarianism'. Calls for a dictatorial approach to achieving sustainability, which were muted in any case, faded with the development of a vibrant green movement, the rise of Green parties, and the commitment they represent to democratic politics. This approach is now so embedded that it is hard to imagine a revival of eco-authoritarianism, despite the sense of urgency that emanates from recent climate science reports. There continues, though, to be a mismatch between the seriousness of these reports and the political response. Right now it is hard to imagine Green parties becoming the mass parties that conservatism, Christian democracy, labour, and social democracy have produced over the past hundred years. In part this is because, to date, mainstream parties have managed to deal with the environmental challenge relatively successfully in the sense of persuading voters that a dedicated alternative is not required. It is also because Green parties have yet to shake off entirely the impression that they are single issue parties, concerned with the environment and nothing else. Although this is not true, and although Green parties can continually assert that a healthy environment is a precondition for everything else anyway, this makes them less attractive than mainstream alternatives when it comes to voters' concerns around the economy, housing, education, and so on.

The one imponderable, the thing that could shake this apparently stable consensus, is that which brought about environmental politics in the first place—the state of the environment itself. Some of the most systematic attempts to measure our progress towards sustainability suggest that we are heading in the wrong direction. We have already mentioned the IPCC and the Millennium Development Goals in this connection. We might add recent work on 'planetary boundaries' by Johann Rockström and his colleagues at the Stockholm Resilience Centre to this—work which suggests that four of the nine boundaries they identify have already been transgressed: climate change, the rate of biodiversity loss, land use, and the rate of interference with the nitrogen cycle. The other boundaries they assess are ocean acidification, freshwater, ozone depletion, atmospheric aerosols, and chemical pollution. The report is a reminder that, although climate change is at present the overriding environmental concern to the degree that environmental politics is practically synonymous with climate politics, there are many more issues besides. Studies like these have the potential to be political game-changers, but they will only realize this potential if and when their implications become part of the lived experience of masses of people with the capacity to organize politically, make demands, and challenge the system that produces unsustainability and inequality.

Environmental politics has a habit of throwing up surprises—who would have thought in the mid-1970s, when there was a surge of interest in 'global cooling', that forty years later environmental politics would be dominated by global warming? One thing, though, is certain: environmental issues are firmly established in the political landscape, and will remain there for a long time to come.

References

Introduction: what is environmental politics?

The Findhorn Foundation website can be found at <http://www.findhorn.org/>.

Nanhe's story appears in 'Dams, Displacement, Policy and Law in India', <http://planningcommission.nic.in/reports/articles/ncsxna/art_dam.pdf>.

Chapter 1: Origins

R. Carson, *Silent Spring* (Boston: Houghton Mifflin, 1962).

R. Inglehart explains his post-material thesis in *The Silent Revolution: Changing Values and Political Styles among Western Publics* (Princeton, NJ: Princeton University Press, 1977).

Chapter 2: Ideas

D. Meadows, D. Meadows, J. Randers, and W. Behrens III, *The Limits to Growth* (New York: Universe Books, 1972).

G. Hardin, 'Lifeboat Ethics: The Case Against Helping the Poor', *Psychology Today* (September 1974). Available at <http://www.garretthardinsociety.org/articles/art_lifeboat_ethics_case_against_helping_poor.html>.

World Commission on Environment and Development, *Our Common Future* (Oxford: Oxford University Press, 1987). Available at <http://www.un-documents.net/our-common-future.pdf>.

P. Singer, *Animal Liberation: A New Ethics for Our Treatment of Animals* (New York: Harper Collins, 1975).

T. Regan, *The Case for Animal Rights* (Oakland: University of California Press, 1983).

The Great Ape Project's website, with details of the project's mission, its news, and sanctuaries, can be found at <http://www.projetogap.org.br/en/>.

A. Naess, 'The Shallow and the Deep, Long-Range Ecology Movement: A Summary', *Inquiry* 16/1 (1973). Available at <http://www.ecology.ethz.ch/education/Readings_stuff/Naess_1973.pdf>.

Quotation is from J. Martínez-Alier, *The Environmentalism of the Poor: A Study of Ecological Conflicts and Valuation* (Cheltenham: Edward Elgar, 2002), p.11.

Quotation is from A. Dobson, *Green Political Thought* (4th edn) (London: Routledge, 2007), pp.2–3.

Quotation is from J. S. Mill, *Principles of Political Economy* (edited and abridged by Stephen Nathanson) (Indianapolis: Hackett Publishing Company, 2004), p.191.

Chapter 3: Movements, parties, policies

Quotation in C. Rootes and R. Brulle, 'Environmental Movements' in D. A. Snow, D. Della Porta, B. Klandermans, and D. McAdam (eds) *The Wiley-Blackwell Encyclopedia of Social and Political Movements* (Chichester: Wiley Blackwell, 2013).

The 2013 survey of the UK environmental movement referred to is J. Cracknell, F. Miller, and H. Williams, *Passionate Collaboration? Taking the Pulse of the UK Environmental Sector*, available at <http://www.greenfunders.org/wp-content/uploads/Passionate-Collaboration-Full-Report.pdf>.

R. Inglehart explains his post-material thesis in *The Silent Revolution: Changing Values and Political Styles among Western Publics* (Princeton, NJ: Princeton University Press, 1977).

M. Diani and P. Donati's framework is Table 1 from 'Organisational Change in Western European Environmental Groups: A Framework for Analysis', *Environmental Politics* 8/1 (1999): 13–34, reproduced by kind permission of Taylor and Francis Ltd (see <http://www.tandfonline.com>).

The Transition Town network has a website at <https://www.transitionnetwork.org/>.

The Green party elections table is inspired by N. Carter, *The Politics of the Environment: Ideas, Activism, Policy* (2nd edn) (Cambridge University Press: Cambridge, 2007), p.89. This version is fully updated and it adds data on some non-European parties and on the most recent available election in each country. The data come from a variety of sources, but Wikipedia is always up to date.

Garrett Hardin's essay on the common-pool resource problem is 'The Tragedy of the Commons', *Science* 162/3859 (1968). It can be found at <http://www.sciencemag.org/content/162/3859/1243.full>.

The UK government's guidance on biodiversity offsetting is at <https://www.gov.uk/biodiversity-offsetting>.

The seven population segments, representing different levels of commitment to pro-environmental behaviour, are described in *A Framework for Pro-Environmental Behaviours* (2008), p.8: <https://www.gov.uk/government/uploads/system/uploads/ attachment_data/file/69277/pb13574-behaviours-report-080110.pdf>.

Chapter 4: Local and global, North and South

B. McKibbin, *The End of Nature* (New York: Anchor, 1989), p.59.

David Held defines globalization in 'Globalization, Corporate Practice and Cosmopolitan Social Standards', *Contemporary Political Theory* 1/1 (2002), p.61.

Vandana Shiva's comment on the asymmetry of globalization processes is in 'The Greening of Global Reach', in G. O. Thuathail, S. Dalby, and P. Routledge (eds), *The Geopolitics Reader* (London: Routledge, 1988), p.233.

Data for the country-by-country CO_2 emissions per capita in Table 2 come from the *Millennium Development Goals Indicators* (2013) at <http://mdgs.un.org/unsd/mdg/SeriesDetail.aspx?srid=751>.

The definition of 'biosecurity' is from A. Dobson, K. Barker, and S. L. Taylor (eds), *Biosecurity: The Socio-Politics of Invasive Species and Infectious Diseases* (London: Earthscan, 2013), p.5.

The Brundtland Commission's famous definition of 'sustainable development' is in *Our Common Future* (Oxford: Oxford University Press, 1987). Available at <http://www.un-documents. net/our-common-future.pdf> (chapter 2, part 1).

The data for the Multilateral Environmental Agreements Table 3 are drawn from a number of sources. A useful starting point is at <http:// en.wikipedia.org/wiki/List_of_international_environmental_ agreements>.

B. Lomborg, *The Skeptical Environmentalist* (Cambridge: Cambridge University Press, 2001).

The information in Box 1 is drawn from the Intergovernmental Panel on Climate Change (IPCC) 'Summary for Policymakers', <https://www.ipcc.ch/pdf/assessment-report/ar5/wg1/WGIAR5_SPM_brochure_en.pdf>. Although the document is dated 2013 it relates to the IPCC's most recent 2014 report.

The warming scenarios table (Table 4) comes from *Warming World: Impacts by Degree* (based on the National Research Council report, *Climate Stabilization Targets: Emissions, Concentrations, and Impacts over Decades to Millennia*, 2011), p.14, at <http://dels.nas.edu/resources/static-assets/materials-based-on-reports/booklets/warming_world_final.pdf>. Reprinted with permission from *Warming World: Impacts by Degree* (based on the National Research Council report, *Climate Stabilization Targets: Emissions, Concentrations, and Impacts over Decades to Millennia*, 2011), by the National Academy of Sciences, Courtesy of the National Academies Press, Washington, D.C.

CO_2 concentrations are tracked on a daily basis at the Mauna Loa observatory in Hawaii: <http://co2now.org/Current-CO2/CO2-Now/global-co2-board.html>.

The UK Met Office's scenario for the effects of 4°C of warming is at <http://www.metoffice.gov.uk/climate-guide/climate-change/impacts/four-degree-rise/map>.

Lumumba Di-Aping and Jon Sauven's comments were quoted in 'Low Targets, Goals Dropped: Copenhagen Ends in Failure', *The Guardian* (19 December 2009), <http://www.theguardian.com/environment/2009/dec/18/copenhagen-deal>.

The Global Carbon Project's website is at <http://www.globalcarbon-project.org/>.

The United Nations Environment Programme (UNEP) document on 'Local Authorities' Initiatives in Support of Agenda 21' can be seen at <http://www.unep.org/documents.multilingual/default.asp?DocumentID=52&ArticleID=76&l=en>.

There is a two-minute video of the underwater Maldive ministers' cabinet meeting at <http://news.bbc.co.uk/1/hi/8311838.stm>.

Friends of the River Narmada have their website at <http://www.narmada.org/>.

Chapter 5: Environmental futures

The Colin Tudge quotation is from *The Time before History: 5 Million Years of Human Impact* (New York: Touchstone, 1997), p.353.

Details of the International Commission on Stratigraphy's working group on the Anthropocene can be found at <http://quaternary.stratigraphy.org/workinggroups/anthropocene/>.

Paul Crutzen and Eugene Stoermer's original article on the Anthropocene, 'The "Anthropocene"', *Global Change Newsletter* 41 (May 2000) is at <http://www.igbp.net/download/18.3 16f18321323470177580001401/NL41.pdf>.

The Millennium Development Goals Report for 2014 is at <http://www.un.org/millenniumgoals/2014%20MDG%20report/MDG%202014%20English%20web.pdf>.

The idea of 'contraction and convergence' was originally developed by Aubrey Meyer of the Global Commons Institute (GCI) in connection with climate change policy. The GCI website has more detail on the idea: <http://www.gci.org.uk/>.

Oxford University has a major geo-engineering research programme. Examples of possible large-scale interventions in the Earth's natural systems can be found on the programme's website at <http://www.geoengineering.ox.ac.uk/>.

The details of how much fossil fuel must remain unused if we are to have a 50 percent chance of keeping warming to below a 2°C increase on pre-industrial levels are in C. McGlade and P. Ekins, 'The Geographical Distribution of Fossil Fuels Unused when Limiting Global Warming to 2°C', *Nature* 517 (January 2015).

The 'Research and Degrowth' definition of degrowth is from the Association's website: <http://www.degrowth.org/definition-2>.

The Stockholm Resilience Centre's work on planetary boundaries is at <http://www.stockholmresilience.org/21/research/research-programmes/planetary-boundaries.html>.

Further reading

Introduction: what is environmental politics?

There are two detailed introductions to environmental politics:
Neil Carter, *The Politics of the Environment: Ideas, Activism, Policy*
(2nd edn) (Cambridge: Cambridge University Press, 2007); and
James Connelly, Graham Smith, David Benson, and Clare
Saunders, *Politics and the Environment: From Theory to Practice*
(3rd edn) (Abingdon: Routledge, 2012). A briefer introduction is
Robert Garner, *Environmental Politics: The Age of Climate Change*
(3rd edn) (Houndmills: Palgrave Macmillan, 2011); and a racier,
more partisan introduction is Derek Wall, *The No-Nonsense Guide
to Green Politics* (Oxford: New Internationalist Publications, 2010).
Two comprehensive 'readers' are: Mark Smith (ed.) *Thinking
Through the Environment: A Reader* (London: Routledge, 1999);
and John Dryzek and David Schlosberg, *Debating the Earth: The
Environmental Politics Reader* (2nd edn) (Oxford: Oxford
University Press, 2005).

Chapter 1: Origins

Clive Ponting, *A Green History of the World: The Environment and the
Collapse of Great Civilisations* (London: Penguin, 1991); and Derek
Wall, *Green History: A Reader in Environmental Literature,
Philosophy and Politics* (London: Routledge, 1994) are excellent
companions. Other books dealing with origins, history, and prospects
are: Ronald Wright, *A Short History of Progress* (Toronto: Anans,
2004); Jared Diamond, *Collapse: How Societies Choose to Fail or
Survive* (London: Allen Lane, 2005); and Donald Worster, *Nature's*

Economy: A History of Ecological Ideas (Cambridge: Cambridge University Press, 1995).

Chapter 2: Ideas

Andrew Dobson, *Green Political Thought* (4th edn) (London: Routledge, 2007), John Barry *Environment and Social Theory* (London: Routledge, 2007), and Tim Hayward, *Political Theory and Ecological Values* (Cambridge: Polity Press, 1998) are three accessible introductions to the themes of this chapter. John Dryzek, *The Politics of the Earth* (3rd edn) (Oxford: Oxford University Press, 2013) is also influential. Donella Meadows, Jorgen Randers, and Dennis Meadows, *Limits to Growth: The 30-Year Update* (London: Earthscan, 2004) is the updated 'limits' thesis, straight from the horse's mouth. Three comprehensive introductions to environmental ethics are: Patrick Curry, *Environmental Ethics: An Introduction* (2nd edn) (Cambridge: Polity Press, 2011); John Benson, *Environmental Ethics: An Introduction with Readings* (London: Routledge, 2000); and Joseph des Jardins, *Environmental Ethics: An Introduction to Environmental Philosophy* (5th edn) (New York: Wadsworth, 2013). Novels include: Ernest Callenbach, *Ecotopia* (Berkeley: Banyan Tree Books, 2004); Aldous Huxley, *Island* (New York: Harper and Brothers, 1962); and Daniel Quinn, *Ishmael* (New York: Bantam Double Day, 1992). The science fiction film *Silent Running* (1972) explores a number of the ethical issues discussed in this chapter.

Chapter 3: Movements, parties, policies

Good places to start for the environmental movement are Brian Doherty, 'Environmental Movements' in Chukwumerije Okereke (ed.) *The Politics of the Environment* (London: Routledge, 2007); and Christopher Rootes, 'Environmental Movements', in David Snow, Sarah Soule, and Hanspeter Kriesi (eds) *Blackwell Companion to New Social Movements* (Oxford: Blackwell, 2004).

Clare Saunders, *Environmental Networks and Social Movement Theory* (London: Bloomsbury, 2013), offers a scholarly treatment, while Brian Doherty and Tim Doyle, *Environmentalism, Resistance and Solidarity: The Politics of Friends of the Earth International* (Houndmills: Palgrave Macmillan, 2013), look at the environmental movement in a transnational context. Edward Abbey's classic novel,

The Monkey-Wrench Gang (London: Penguin, 2004), explores the themes of environmental activism and sabotage. E. Gene Frankland, Paul Lucardie, and Benoît Rihoux (eds) *Green Parties in Transition: The End of Grass-Roots Democracy?* (Farnham: Ashgate, 2008) is a comprehensive collection of essays on Green parties from around the world. Ferdinand Müller-Rommel and Thomas Poguntke (eds) *Green Parties in National Governments* (London: Frank Cass, 2002) look at the experience of Green parties in government. Good introductions to environmental policy-making include: Carolyn Snell and Gary Haq, *The Short Guide to Environmental Policy* (Bristol: Policy Press, 2014); and Jane Roberts, *Environmental Policy* (2nd edn) (Abingdon: Routledge, 2011). Julian Agyeman links environmental policy-making and social justice in *Introducing Just Sustainabilities: Policy, Planning and Practice* (London: Zed Books, 2013).

Chapter 4: Local and global, North and South

Peter Christoff and Robyn Eckersley, *Globalization and the Environment* (Maryland: Rowman and Littlefield, 2013), James Evans, *Environmental Governance* (Abingdon: Routledge, 2011), Elizabeth DeSombre, *The Global Environment and World Politics* (London: Continuum, 2007), and Peter Dauvergne (ed.), *Handbook of Global Environmental Politics* (2nd edn) (Cheltenham: Edward Elgar, 2012) all cover environment and sustainability as global issues. There is a more detailed look at regional environmental policy in Andrew Jordan and Camilla Adelle (eds) *Environmental Policy in the EU: Actors, Institutions and Processes* (2nd edn) (Abingdon: Earthscan/Routledge, 2011). Hayley Stevenson and John Dryzek look at the challenge of reaching a lasting international climate agreement in *Democratising Global Climate Governance* (Cambridge: Cambridge University Press, 2014), while John Vogler's *Climate Change and World Politics* (London: Palgrave/Macmillan, 2015) sets the evolution of the climate change debate in its wider international context and investigates questions of national interest, recognition, and climate justice. Joan Martínez Alier's *Environmentalism of the Poor* (Cheltenham: Edward Elgar, 2002) is a classic on environmental justice, while David Schlosberg links justice, nature, and environmental movements in *Defining Environmental Justice: Theories, Movements, and Nature* (Oxford: Oxford University Press, 2007). Barbara Kingsolver's *Flight Behaviour* (London: HarperCollins, 2013) is a brilliant novel about science and climate change.

Chapter 5: Environmental futures

Among the key contributions to post-growth and degrowth are: Richard Heinberg, *Peak Everything: Waking Up to the Century of Decline in Earth's Resources* (Clairview: Forest Row, 2007); Tim Jackson, *Prosperity Without Growth* (Abingdon: Routledge, 2009); Rob Dietz and Dan O'Neill, *Enough is Enough* (Abingdon: Earthscan/ Routledge, 2013); and Serge Latouche, *Farewell to Growth* (Cambridge: Polity, 2009). A less doom-laden account of the implications of the Anthropocene can be found in Gaia Vince's *Adventures in the Anthropocene: A Journey to the Heart of the Planet We Made* (London: Chatto and Windus, 2014). Ecological modernization is well covered in Arthur Mol, David Sonnerfeld, and Gert Spaargaren (eds) *The Ecological Modernisation Reader: Environmental Reform in Theory and Practice* (Abingdon: Routledge, 2010).

William Ophuls' *Ecology and the Politics of Scarcity Revisited: The Unraveling of the American Dream* (New York: W. H. Freeman, 1992) and *Plato's Revenge* (Cambridge, MA: MIT Press, 2011) deal elegantly with the challenge to democracy. Among the many fictional treatments of environmental futures are: Howard Kunstler, *A World Made by Hand* (New York: Atlantic Monthly Press, 2008); Margaret Atwood's trilogy, *Oryx and Crake* (2003), *The Year of the Flood* (2009), and *MaddAddam* (2013) (all London: Bloomsbury Press); Paolo Bacigalupi, *The Windup Girl* (London: Orbit, 2010); and Nathaniel Rich, *Odds Against Tomorrow* (New York: Farrar, Straus and Giroux, 2013).

Index

SOCIAL MEDIA
Very Short Introduction

Join our community

www.oup.com/vsi

- Join us online at the official Very Short Introductions **Facebook** page.
- Access the thoughts and musings of our authors with our online **blog**.
- Sign up for our monthly **e-newsletter** to receive information on all new titles publishing that month.
- Browse the full range of Very Short Introductions online.
- Read **extracts** from the Introductions for free.
- Visit our library of **Reading Guides**. These guides, written by our expert authors will help you to question again, why you think what you think.
- If you are a teacher or lecturer you can order inspection copies quickly and simply via our website.

ONLINE CATALOGUE
A Very Short Introduction

Our online catalogue is designed to make it easy to find your ideal Very Short Introduction. View the entire collection by subject area, watch author videos, read sample chapters, and download reading guides.

http://fds.oup.com/www.oup.co.uk/general/vsi/index.html